TOUCHDOWNS TIPOFFS & TESTIMONIES

A Look at the Spiritual Side of BYU Athletics

By Floyd Johnson
With Val Hale

ALBA PUBLISHING
Orem, Utah

To Hannah and Nancy

ISBN 0-8425-2387-1

First Printing, 1989

Printed in the United States of America
Photography by Mark Philbrick
Cover Design by Shari Warnick

FOREWORD

Occasionally, individuals collaborate, and the results of the enterprise are magical. The publication you are about to read is a prime example of that statement. The most successful partnerships are those where each of the partners have strengths that supplement the other.

Val Hale is a gifted writer. He is an idea man. He is visionary in many respects. His sincere interest in competitive athletics and in young men resulted in his insistence that Floyd Johnson begin to catalogue and publish his experiences with BYU athletes. Val had the dream—Floyd makes dreams come true.

Floyd Johnson, the other half of the collaboration, is one of the finest men on planet earth. He is one of the most Christian individuals in my acquaintanceship. He believes that "inasmuch as ye have done it unto one of the least of these my brethren, ye have done it unto me." Floyd Johnson is a listener. Floyd Johnson is a teacher. Floyd Johnson is a counselor. Floyd Johnson is a "fixer."

As equipment manager for the Department of Athletics at Brigham Young University for over 35 years, Floyd has repaired every type of equipment used in athletics. Some of his work is masterful. His best repair jobs, however, have taken place with broken hearts, with frayed feelings, with disappointed performers, and with repentant souls. The results of his work are best seen in the lives of literally thousands of young men and women who have come under his guidance and tutelage. Floyd has a baccalaureate degree in business. More importantly, he has an informal Ph.D. in the field of human relationships. He is in every sense of the word a physician who administers to the personal needs of all with whom he comes in contact.

The stories are true, the characters are real, the results have been almost unbelievable. If you like athletics, if you admire young people, if you believe in magic—read on.

Glen Tuckett
BYU Athletic Director

Prologue

Thirty-one years ago I came to Brigham Young University as the athletic equipment manager. My job has consisted mainly of keeping BYU's athletes outfitted in clean, safe uniforms. I wash their clothes every day. I sew numbers on their jerseys. I fix their broken helmets and find shoes to fit their oversized feet.

As jobs go, mine probably isn't the most glamorous on campus. In fact, if I weren't working with some of the finest young people in the world, I probably would have switched professions long ago. But the thing that has kept me going all these years is the chance to share the gospel with the thousands of athletes who have played for BYU. I guess you could say I'm the team evangelist. I've spent countless hours sharing my testimony with non-member athletes and counseling LDS young men who are struggling with decisions of missions, marriage, and life.

It's never easy to mix religion and athletics—even at BYU. When I came to BYU years ago, I found a football program I was entirely ashamed of. Most of the coaches were non-members and were not interested in promoting the school's ideals. And most of the LDS coaches were not active Church members.

Occasionally, I would hear football players bragging about their escapades on road trips. They would go to bed with their clothes on, and, after the coaches made their bed checks, they would throw off their covers and go out on the town. When the players got back to Provo, they would boast of where they had been and what they had done. Not all the players did that, but many of them did, and I was disappointed. To me, athletics was a means of teaching the gospel, but we certainly weren't doing much missionary work in our football program.

One day I was talking to R.K. Brown, a football player from Georgia. He was a convert to the Church, and I was asking him about his conversion. As I was speaking with him, I felt the presence of someone coming up behind me. I didn't look to see who it was; I just kept talking. When we finished our conversation, I walked into the equipment room. The person who had been standing behind me followed me into my office. I turned around and saw that it was one of the assistant coaches, an inactive Mormon.

"Coach, can I do something for you?" I asked.

"Yes," he answered. "Did I hear you talking to Brown out there about religion?"

I said, "Well, he was telling me about his conversion to the Church."

He stared at me, and then, with an angry voice, said, "I'm going to give you a piece of advice. You keep your mouth shut when it comes to the Church. You were never hired to be a missionary. You were hired to be a jock washer." He walked away and left me standing with my mouth open.

I really anguished that night about what he said. In fact, my wife got out of bed and slept in the front room because I was tossing and turning so much. But by morning, I had my mind made up about a few things. One was that the assistant football coach hadn't hired me. The other was that the athletic director and the dean of the college, who did hire me, had never told me what I could or could not say as far as the Church was concerned. And until they did, I was going to say anything I wanted to say that would build the Church and build faith in the lives of these athletes, particularly the football team.

One by one, I picked out the players I wanted to proselyte, and I couldn't wait to get to football practice that afternoon because I was going to let those guys share my testimony.

At the end of that season, the football coaches, including the assistant coach who confronted me, were fired. Only Tally Stevens was retained from that staff, and he became the head coach. Since that time, I have shared my testimony with hundreds of athletes—many of whom have joined the Church.

Also in that day and age, returned missionaries were not a welcome addition to our football team. Most missionaries who left the football program to serve missions never came back to play. The football coaches made them feel so bad they didn't want to come back. It wasn't until LaVell Edwards became football coach in 1972 that returned missionaries were accepted as part of our football program. In 1984, the year BYU won the football National Championship, there were 52 returned missionaries on our team.

During my years at BYU, I've seen the attitude on the football and basketball programs gradually change to where the teams' spiritual quality allows the athletes to carry the gospel with them wherever they go. Occasionally they slip a little, but I strongly believe the athletic department has a mandate to carry the message of the gospel wherever it goes—to member and non-member alike.

Ever since that assistant football coach tried to re-write my job description, I have seen many miracles take place in the lives of young men. I have shared these wonderful stories in countless firesides, hoping they might kindle a divine spark in the soul of someone struggling with a testimony. After much persuasion by friends—and hesitation and reluctance on my part—I agreed to publish these experiences so they might be shared by many people. My prayer is that, by reading some of these true stories, young people and adults will be inspired to live better lives.

Tackling the Gospel

People often ask, "How many athletes have you converted?" I always respond that I haven't converted anyone. It was the Apostle Paul who said, "I have planted,
Apollos watered; but God gave the increase" (1 Corinthians
3:6). All credit for any conversions must go to Heavenly
Father and to the Lord because they are the ones who really
bring about the conversion of souls into the Church. The rest
of us can plant the seed, and we can water; but nearly every
young man or young woman who has been baptized has had
many wonderful people play a part in that baptism. Coaches,
teammates, girlfriends, boyfriends, and teachers provide
wonderful examples for and have a powerful influence on
these young people who decide to take upon themselves the
name of Christ.

Hundreds of non-Mormon athletes have attended BYU
over the years. Typically, they are outstanding young men

and women with high standards who are seeking a quality
education in a wholesome environment while they participate
in their respective sports. A few come to BYU solely to
participate in athletics and to use their college experience as
a stepping stone to professional sports. Some come to BYU
not fully understanding what is required of them when they
sign the "honor code"; nevertheless, they adjust, finish their
sports careers, and move on to become successful citizens.

But whatever their background and whatever their motive
for attending BYU, these athletes eventually come face to
face with Mormonism. I have enjoyed watching their en-
counters with LDS culture. Reactions have varied from
complete acceptance of the gospel to total rejection of everything having to do with religion. Many have sincerely studied
the LDS faith without ever converting to Mormonism. Others
are as interested in religion as they are in running wind sprints,
and the only religion classes they attend are those that are
required to keep them academically eligible. Quite a few
non-Mormon athletes have left BYU impressed with the
Church and have been baptized later in their lives.

* * *

I'll always remember Keith Rivera, a bruiser who came out
of Las Vegas, Nevada, back in the early 1970s. He was
practically raised in the gambling casinos because his father
was a card dealer.

Keith came to BYU to play football. He was a big,
defensive lineman, and he hadn't even finished his freshman
year before acquiring the nickname "Mad Dog." He simply
could not get along with other people. Defensive linemen
generally are not noted for their manners and congeniality,
but Keith was particularly unsociable.

Before the season was over, he asked if he could have his
locker moved to another area of the locker room. He said he
didn't like the guys he was dressing by. I imagine they teased

him a lot because he was antagonistic. So I said, "Sure, Keith, I can move you out. I can let you dress in the back room with the gymnasts. But the lockers in there are much smaller, and I'll have to give you two. You'll have to remember two combinations instead of one."

"Anything to get away from those guys," he said.

So I moved him into the big dressing room in the back with the gymnasts and the wrestlers and the baseball players. And that's where he dressed until the spring of his junior year. During that time, I noticed a slow change take place in Keith's life. It was so slow that very few people noticed it. But I did.

He came in to see me at the beginning of spring football his junior year and asked if he could move back into his old locker. "Sure," I said. "No one has used that locker since we moved you out. I've left it empty because I knew someday you would want it back."

I don't know where Keith went that summer, but I didn't see him again until the middle of August. I was seated at the sewing machine working on some football jerseys when Keith walked in. I glanced up and saw this giant of a man standing there looking at me.

"Floyd," he said in a serious voice, "I'm ready to change. I want you to know that I'm just like putty. Mold me any way you want to mold me."

I just sat there staring at that big defensive end, wondering if what I was hearing was for real. Was this "Mad Dog" talking? Obviously, something had happened to him over the summer. And from that moment on, he was receptive to everything I told him about the gospel. Before he could change his mind, I got him taking the missionary lessons.

About the third game that year, Keith hurt his ankle. Dr. Vance, the team doctor, gave him two choices: one was that he could have an operation—which he was going to need eventually—and sit out the rest of the season; the other option was that he could receive a shot of novocaine into his injured ankle before each game. That way he would be able to play until the season ended and then have the operation.

Keith chose the novocaine.

The first game we played after his injury was a home game. I remember standing in the training room watching Keith lying on the table with his ankle exposed. Dr. Vance hovered over him with a syringe and a big needle that must have been three inches long. Standing around Keith were guys like Wayne Baker, Stan Varner, Paul Linford, and Orrin Olsen, who were there to give him moral support.

Stan Varner was the first to say something. He looked at Keith and said, "If you'll take hold of our hands and squeeze for all you're worth when Dr. Vance inserts that needle, you'll never feel a thing."

Keith grabbed their hands and squeezed until I thought the bones might break. I saw his hand go white from the pressure of those big, strong hands that were constricting his. As I looked up at the faces of Keith's teammates, they were grimacing with pain. Then I looked at "Mad Dog" Rivera. He was lying there with a sweet smile on his face while Dr. Vance inserted that needle into his ankle.

That same scene occurred seven more times. Seven times that year those guys shared Keith's pain. They were there to support their friend and brother. To me, that was one of the greatest displays of teamwork I've ever seen.

That was in 1974, the year BYU won the Western Athletic Conference and went to the Fiesta Bowl—the school's very first bowl game.

Keith soon was baptized a member of the Church. He hung around a few years after that because he got married and waited for his wife to graduate. The last I saw of "Mad Dog," he was living in Oregon. He dropped in once on the way to a funeral. When I saw him, I said to myself, "To really get conversion into the Church, you must have love for the person you're trying to convert. And you've got to show that love so he will understand you are sincere in what you're trying to do. Those big, tough defensive linemen had succeeded in loving Keith into the Church."

* * *

Kenny Bray played football for BYU back when losing to Utah by less than two touchdowns was considered a "moral victory." He was a linebacker from Calgary, Canada.

One Friday night I was shopping with my wife at a super-market near our home in Orem. I was pushing a cart, and she was filling it with food as we strolled up and down the aisles. I glanced up and noticed several big guys near the walk-in box, but I didn't pay much attention to them. As we got closer, however, I recognized one of them as Kenny Bray. He was with two or three other football players. I decided to bump them with my cart just for a little fun, but then I noticed they were filling their cart with beer.

"I don't want to get caught in this trap," I thought to myself, and I hurried down the next aisle without being seen.

The supermarket was located in the boundaries of the ward where I was then serving as bishop, and several of the priests in my ward worked as bag boys at the store. When my wife and I reached the checkout counter, I asked one of the boys if the football players had come through yet.

"Yea," he said. "They had a whole cart full of beer. I asked what they were going to do with it, and they said they were going to use it to wash their hair."

I was really troubled because when I started working at BYU, I had been told that I was to watch the players. If I saw any standards violations, I was to report them. The same thing was expected of all athletic administrators. I lay awake all that night worrying about what I should do.

The next morning we had an indoor track meet. Back then, athletes could work for $15 a month spending money. We called it grant-in-aid. Kenny Bray was on a grant-in-aid, and that morning I had him assigned to help Coach Clarence Robison get ready for the track meet.

Kenny showed up at quarter to seven. I looked him in the eye and said, "You know, Kenny, I didn't sleep last night because of you."

Surprised, he said, "Because of me?"

"Yes, because of you."

"Why would I cause you to lose any sleep?" he asked.

I told him how I had been at the supermarket and had seen him and the other players loading their cart with beer. Then, with determination in my voice, I said, "Now I have to go see Coach (Tommy) Hudspeth and report you."

Kenny's eyes grew wide, and he said, "No, you didn't see me at the store."

I shook my head, looked him in the eye, and said, "Kenny, I saw you. I was within three or four feet of you, but you were so busy with your beer you didn't notice me. It was eight o'clock. You even told the bag boy you were going to wash your hair with that beer. Now, in order for me to live with myself, I've got to go tell Coach Hudspeth what I know. I don't want to do that, but I've got to."

He looked at me with a horrified expression on his face. "If you tell Coach Hudspeth, I'll lose my scholarship!" he exclaimed.

"That's something you should have thought about last night," I reminded him.

"If I promise that I'll never do it again, wouldn't that be okay?" he begged.

"No," I replied, "because I have already seen you violate the standards. I have to report you. When Coach Hudspeth comes, I'm going to go visit with him. You go on out to the track. Coach Robison is waiting for you."

He left and came back again in 15 minutes. "This is really serious," he said. "If you go tell Coach Hudspeth, I'm going to have to go back home because he'll take my scholarship away."

"Ken, I'm really sorry about that," I responded, "but you have placed me in a position where I have to choose whether I'm going to live with myself or go around feeling guilty and unhappy because I have become a party to your violation of standards. Now you go back out on the track."

About 10 minutes later, I walked down the hallway toward Coach Hudspeth's office. Here came Kenny. "Are you going to see Coach Hudspeth?" he asked in an almost-frantic voice. I hadn't really made up my mind, but I said, "Yep, I'm on my way up there now."

"Floyd, please don't go," he pleaded. "I'll even put my hand on a Bible if you won't go."

"Sorry, I've got to do it," I said.

Then I suddenly got a flash of inspiration—and that doesn't happen to me very often. I said, "Ken, if I was the coach and a player came in and told me he had violated the standards, I'd be a lot easier on him than if someone squealed on him."

"You would?" Kenny asked.

"I sure would. I think Coach Hudspeth is up there right now. Let's go up, and you can tell him what happened."

"Do you really think that would be the best thing to do?" he said.

"Yes, I think that would be the best," I nodded. So we walked up the stairs to the football office. As we reached the top, he stopped.

"I can't do it," he moaned.

"Yes you can," I said. I grabbed him by the arm, opened the door, shoved him inside, shut the door, and held my foot against it so he couldn't get out. By that time Coach Hudspeth had seen him, and it was too late for him to escape.

I didn't see Kenny all the rest of that day, and I worried about him a lot. Then Sunday morning at 7 o'clock he came into my office.

"I suppose you've been wondering what happened," he said. "I went in and told Coach Hudspeth. He made me go around and get all the other guys who were involved, and he placed us on probation. Floyd, I came here this morning because I realize the anguish you were going through trying to decide what to do about me. I have never had anyone show that much concern for me. I came here because I want to thank you for helping me right my life again."

He had tears in his eyes, and I was really happy to see how that potentially damaging situation had been turned into a positive one.

Within six months, Kenny Bray was baptized into the Church. He eventually married a girl from San Juan County. I'll always remember Kenny because he had a size 7 7/8 head, and I had to look everywhere to find a helmet that would fit him. But apparently he had something inside that large head of his because he finally joined the Church. Today he holds high positions of leadership in the Church and works with the youth. He is living life to its fullest because he got caught in a trap at an Orem supermarket many years ago. Love and concern served as the catalyst that ignited a testimony inside his heart.

* * *

Before the revelation about blacks and the priesthood in 1978, very few black athletes attended BYU. Since that time, the number of blacks in all sports at the University has increased. Often it is difficult for them to adjust to the predominantly white Mormon culture in Provo. Yet a few not only have adapted to the LDS lifestyle, but they have also adopted it.

Jeff Chatman, a black, came to Provo in 1984 after the assistant basketball coach, Roger Reid, stumbled onto him at a high school all-star basketball game in Alabama. The Cougars had defeated the University of Alabama-Birmingham the night before in the first round of the NCAA tournament, and Reid decided that watching an all-star game would be better than sitting in the hotel room reading a novel. So he went to the game and was impressed with Chatman's play. Coach Reid eventually convinced Jeff to attend school in far-away Provo.

Chatman soon became a favorite with BYU's fans and coaches. He had a turn-around jump shot that was as smooth, as effortless, and as effective as any I have ever seen. In addition to being a great athlete, he was a great person. He had a smile so bright you almost had to put on sunglasses whenever he flashed it.

I worked on Chatman in a subtle way during the early part of his career. Then, when Jeff was a sophomore, I got a letter from Andy Toolson, a player who had befriended Jeff before leaving on a mission to Chile. Andy had been in the mission field for only a short time, and he told me to tell Jeff to read the *Book of Mormon* because when he got back, he was going to baptize him. I told Chatman about Andy's letter, and he laughed and said, "Oh, when he gets back, I'll be ready."

When Andy came back, he was anxious to meet with Chat and push him toward baptism. At that time, we didn't know the things that were going on in Chat's life. We didn't know his folks opposed his joining the Church and that his family's minister had been giving him a hard time and was fighting mad.

Jason Jackson, a black baseball player, was baptized in November, 1987, and Jeff was scheduled to be baptized then, too. But he backed out at the last minute. A few days after Jason's baptism, I was talking to Jeff and mentioned that I hadn't seen him at the baptismal service.

"I was there," he said, "but I didn't get baptized."

"Will you let me know when you get baptized?" I asked.

"You'll be number one," he assured me.

That afternoon, I was talking to Andy Toolson, and I told him I didn't want to harrass Jeff to the point where he thought my sole ambition in life was to have him baptized. Andy said he had been feeling the same way, so we both agreed to back off.

The very next day, Chat came into my office and said, "Floyd, will you speak at my baptismal service?"

"You're being baptized?" I asked. "Of course I'll speak at your baptismal service."

Jeff had decided to be baptized on a Sunday evening. I drove into the parking lot of the stake center about 15 minutes before the baptism, and I couldn't find a parking place. "They must be having stake conference," I thought. As I stepped into the chapel, I was certain it was stake conference because every seat was taken in the chapel, and people were seated in the overflow. Then I looked up on the stand, and there sat Jeff Chatman all dressed in white. It wasn't stake conference. It was Chatman conference!

I took a seat on the stand, leaned over to Jeff and said, "Are all these people here to see you baptized?"

"I don't know," he shrugged.

"They can only have 75 people in the room by the baptismal font," I reminded him, "so you're going to have to be baptized four times if everyone is going to see you baptized."

Jeff's roommate, also a black, performed the baptism. They took him into to the chapel after the baptism, and Reed Benson gave a talk on the Holy Ghost. Then Ladell Andersen, flanked by all the players and assistant coaches who held the Melchizedek Priesthood, placed their hands upon his head and confirmed him a member of the Church.

It was one of the most touching scenes I can ever remember at a baptismal service. All the returned missionaries on the nationally ranked basketball team were standing there with the coaches, tears running down their cheeks while they confirmed Jeff a member of the Church.

Then they asked Jeff if he wanted to say a few words. He stood up before the crowd of more than 400 and said, "Three and a half years ago, I came to this university and didn't know anybody. I didn't have any friends, and I was alone and scared. Tonight I am baptized a member of the Church, and all you people are here. Are you really my friends?" Then the tears rained down, and he bore his new-found testimony of the Church.

I was chatting with him the following day and asked if his family knew about his baptism. "I'm not going to tell them until I get home because they didn't want me to get baptized," he said. "I'll tell them when I go home for Christmas."

Well, he went home, and when he got back I asked how he had been accepted by his family. He said they were very upset. An article about the BYU team in *USA Today* had mentioned Jeff's baptism. His dad had seen the article and called to see if it was true. Jeff confirmed that he had been baptized and reminded his father that he had mentioned several times his desire to join the LDS Church.

"But we thought you were only kidding," his father responded. He was really upset and informed Jeff that they would not attend the basketball game in Birmingham. He also mentioned that Jeff had turned out to be a big disappointment to their family.

The following week, Jeff's dad called again to ask if he was really happy. "I'm the happiest I've ever been in my life," Jeff responded. "In fact, the only dark cloud hanging over me is the way you and Mom feel."

"Jeff," his dad said, "your mother and I have been talking this thing over, and our main goal in life is your happiness. If you're happy, we're going to be happy. Can you send us 20 tickets to the BYU-UAB game?"

There were about 100 friends and relatives at the game in Birmingham that month. And today Jeff is a happy young man who is thoroughly converted to the Church.

* * *

In 1966 we had three young men come in from California to play football. Their names were Paul Satorius, John Loupoi, and George Gurber. Those three roomed together in Helaman Halls and often got in lengthy discussions about the

Mormon Church. The discussions often would last until the early hours of the morning.

There was one LDS young man in their room, and when they came to a point of doctrine they didn't understand, the LDS boy offered to call the bishop.

"What's a bishop?" the non-members asked.

"He's the leader of the ward," the LDS boy said.

"What's a ward?" they questioned.

Finally, they reached the bishop, who happened to be Jae Ballif, a former BYU football player who later became a mission president and Academic Vice-President of BYU. Sometimes they would call him in the middle of the night, and he would listen patiently to their questions and quietly explain the answers. One night, he said to George Gurber, "Why don't you drop by and see me sometime?"

George was so impressed by Bishop Ballif's courtesy, even when he awoke the Bishop in the middle of the night, that he decided to meet this unusual man. When George finally met Bishop Ballif, he said he had never been accepted so warmly by a stranger as he was on that occasion. That Bishop's kindness made a lasting impression on George and the other two non-members.

George was the son of a Presbyterian minister. When his dad learned George would be coming to BYU where there was no smoking or drinking, where they had bed checks every night at 10:30, he was delighted with his son's choice. In fact, he made the comment, "That's just what George needs!"

George was a big, outspoken kid. It seemed his voice stood out above the others in the locker room and out in the hall.

I grew somewhat weary of hearing him all the time, but he developed into a pretty good football player, and by his junior year he began to mellow just a little bit. He married a gal named Nancy and brought her back to Provo.

During his senior year, George told me he and Nancy didn't want to return to California after graduation. They wanted to stay in Utah and find a job coaching or teaching. He eventually got a job teaching art at Dixon Junior High in Provo for a year before moving to Southern California to take a teaching job at a junior high there.

By that time, George had begun to accept much of Mormonism's doctrine. But Nancy was still skeptical. Whenever possible, George would go into the school's library and read anything he could find about Mormonism—including anti-Mormon books. The negative literature had little effect on George because he had lived with the Mormons, become friends with them, and graduated from their university.

One day, he picked up a tattered, worn book and looked at the title. It was *A Marvelous Work and a Wonder*. He sat in the library, looking through the book and reading it. Then he said, "All of a sudden a beautiful, warm feeling came all over me. I didn't understand it at the time, but I knew it was something good and some kind of sign. I knew that somehow, some way, we were going to have to get in touch with the Mormon Church again."

George and Nancy attended several Presbyterian churches near their home. They even went to his father's church. But they agreed many of the things they heard at those churches couldn't be right. Then one Sunday, George said to Nancy, "Why don't we go to a Mormon church today?" Surprisingly, Nancy was willing to go along.

When they entered the Mormon chapel, they were greeted by friendly people who wanted to know where they were from. "We're from BYU," they said—a statement that didn't seem to cause any unusual attention. Consequently, George went to priesthood meeting, Nancy attended Relief Society, and they both fit in perfectly with the members.

It wasn't until the second or third Sunday that a brother asked George what priesthood he held. "I don't hold any priesthood," George responded. Shocked, the man said, "I thought you said you went to BYU."

"I did go to BYU," George said.

Finally they figured out the Gurbers were not members.

Not long after that, the missionaries began coming, and the Gurbers were converted, along with George's sister.

Seven years ago I got a telephone call from George. He had moved back to Utah and had just been set apart as Elders Quorum president. Several years later I got another call from George. "Floyd," he said, "I had to phone you. I didn't think this would ever happen to me. I bet you can't guess where I've been tonight."

I tried to think of something, but the Church was the farthest thing from my mind. He told me he had been to see the stake president and had been called to be a bishop.

"Isn't that crazy?" he said, "Me, the son of a protestant minister, a Mormon bishop." I assured him that wasn't the first time that had happened.

His father is retired now and comes to Utah often. I asked him once if he thought his father would ever be baptized into the Mormon Church. He smiled and said, "I never thought I was going to be a Mormon bishop."

George's other two roommates also joined the Church. Paul Satorius had an unusual capacity for spiritual things even as a non-member. He eventually was baptized and became a seminary teacher.

Johnny Lupoi married a gal who wasn't LDS. Soon after their wedding, however, they both took the missionary lessons and decided to be baptized. They had a baptismal date set, and I went to the chapel at the prescribed time, but no one was there. I didn't see Johnny for a few days and later learned that his parents had raised a tremendous fuss about his being baptized, even to the point of making threats. They called off the original baptism date and decided to be baptized in a private ceremony a few days later.

* * *

resimir Cosic is a BYU basketball legend. His fancy
passes, unorthodox shots, and on-court antics will never
be forgotten by anyone who saw him perform his magic for
the Cougars.

I first heard of Kresimir Cosic in the late 1960s when Coach
Stan Watts told me he had recruited a big, tall Yugoslavian
who wanted to play fast-break basketball. I didn't know
anything about him. But I remember the day I met him. I
was seated at the sewing machine when Coach Watts brought
him in. I looked up at that kid and didn't think I was ever
going to find the top of his head. He was 6 feet, 11 inches tall
and had coal-black hair that stuck right on top of his head. I
doubt he had a comb or a brush. He probably just ran his hand
through it every morning.

Kresh, as we called him, didn't speak very good English,
and when Coach Watts introduced him to me, I reached out
to shake his hand. He had a big, beautiful smile on his face
and stretched out his massive, ham-like hand, smothering my
little hand with his.

I thought, "Well, if he's communist, he can't be too bad
because that smile of his looks just like someone turned on a
10,000-watt light bulb inside him."

As the year went on, I got to know Kresimir better. I
honestly can't say I was thrilled with his behavior off the
court. In fact, I wasn't so sure I wanted Kresh to return for
his sophomore year. I had some concerns about his commitment to the Honor Code.

But the next year he came back again—with the same,
beautiful smile, wearing the same, size-14 shoe, which up
until that time was the largest shoe any BYU basketball player
had worn. During his sophomore year, I stayed aloof from
him. Then we moved to the Marriott Center before his junior
year.

I went to a store one day to pick up some shoes, and the
manager said, "I hear Kresimir Cosic was baptized."

"Where'd you hear that?" I asked. He told me he had heard it from good authority. "Hey, I know who's baptized and who isn't at BYU," I said. "That guy will *never* be baptized, and if he is, the water will never stop boiling."

I returned to the Marriott Center to get ready for practice, and I could hear Rod Kimball, the team trainer, and Kresimir chatting in the training room. Kresimir said to Rod: "What you do if I tell you that I be Mormon?"

Rod laughed and said, "Kresh, if you ever get to be a Mormon, I'll apostatize."

Kresimir glowed one of his big smiles and said, "Rod, one thing we Mormons don't like is man who say he do something and then not do it."

After Kresh went out on the floor, Rod and I discussed his alleged baptism. I mentioned to Rod what the store manager had told me and asked if he thought it was true. "I don't think anybody could baptize him," he laughed.

We eventually spoke with the custodian at the Jesse Knight Building, where they hold baptisms on campus, and we learned that, indeed, Kresimir had been baptized a few days earlier.

"Who would baptize him?" I wondered aloud. We were both stunned to learn that Hugh B. Nibley, probably the smartest man at BYU, had been so dumb as to baptize Kresimir Cosic. Well, we didn't say anything, we just sat back to observe Kresimir.

Not long after that, I slipped into the dressing room to talk to the guys. Some of the players were in there making off-color remarks that were crude and inappropriate. Kresimir stepped into the room just in time to hear what they said. He walked over to the players who had been making the vulgar remarks and said, "In this dressing room, we don't talk like that."

The player looked up at him with astonishment because Kresh usually was the ring leader in that kind of conversation. But now he was calling them to repentance because they were telling off-color stories in the locker room. I just sat back and smiled, wondering if this was all for real, if Kresimir really had made a change.

The next year, Kresh didn't show up for practice one day, so Coach Potter asked me to see if he was in the dressing room. I pushed open the dressing room door, and there stood Kresh. He still had his pants on, but his shirt was off. I noticed he was wearing temple garments. He just stood there looking into the mirror, admiring them as if he were someone trying on fine, new clothing for the first time.

I didn't want to intrude, so I let the door shut. Then I hit it with my hand so he would know I was coming in. He turned around, looked at me and said, "See my new clothes? My beautiful clothes."

"Kresh, you've been to the temple," I said.

He smiled and looked back into the mirror. "Yes. I've been to the temple. Don't you think my clothes are beautiful?"

I knew a conversion had taken place.

Then I remembered a scripture where the Lord is speaking to the prophet Jeremiah. He says, "Behold, I will make a new covenant with the house of Israel ... I will put my law in their inward parts, and write it in their hearts; and I will be their God, and they shall be my people" (Jeremiah 31: 31-33). I also thought of the scripture where Isaiah prophesies, "And he will lift up an ensign to the nations from afar ..." (Isaiah 5:26).

That is what has become of Kresimir Cosic. He has become an ensign to all nations. This great man who came here to play fast-break basketball has turned out to be a fast-break missionary.

That first year after his conversion, Kresimir came to me and, in his deep, accented voice, said, "Floyd, I want all shirts that say Brigham Young." I told him that the only shirts I had were the old ones I had collected to give to the custodians for rags. But he said, "If they say Brigham Young, I take."

So I gathered up all the old T-shirts I could find and shipped them to Yugoslavia. It cost us $75 to send them. I had no idea what he planned to do with them.

I later found out that in Yugoslavia he was like the Pied Piper. All the kids followed him around wherever he went. He had his testimony printed on little sheets of paper and the articles of faith translated into Serbo Croatian, the Yugoslav language. As he walked down the street, little kids would come up to him and say, "Kresh, I want a shirt just like yours."

Kresimir would pull out a card and say, "If you will memorize what's on that card, I will give you a T-shirt just like mine."

The communist leaders must have loved him for doing that. When I found out what he was doing, that was the last time I sent him old T-shirts. From then on, I sent only new ones. You couldn't do that today because of NCAA restrictions, but back then it wasn't a problem.

Kresimir eventually became a district president in Yugo-slavia. Once each year, I would receive his district paper, telling of the events that had taken place behind the Iron Curtain. Misho Ostarsavic, another young man who played basketball here and was converted by Kresimir, is a branch president in Yugoslavia. His wife is the Relief Society pres-ident.

Most people know about the conversion of the Apostle Paul. They are also familiar with the conversion of Alma and the Sons of Mosiah. But, to me, Kresimir's conversion supercedes those because he was from a communist country and knew little about God, Jesus, or any Christian religion. He had been taught all his life that there was no such thing as a God. But Hugh Nibley had been smart enough to teach him and to baptize him a member of the Church.

About once a year Kresimir comes back to Provo. I still keep a pair of size-14 basketball shoes hidden away so he can work out. He goes to the temple, and people up there still remember him and love to take care of him. He is one of the real miracle conversions that have taken place here at Brigham Young University.

* * *

These are only a few of the hundreds of athletes who have tackled the gospel at BYU. I could fill several volumes with similar stories of young men and women who have entered the waters of baptism. The miracle of conversion has become a common occurrence on this campus. And as long as we have our priorities in the right place, the miracle will only become more evident.

2

Long and Deep

O ne of the most spectacular plays in football is the long, deep forward pass. From the time the ball spirals from the quarterback's hand until it is hopefully grabbed by the receiver, fans, players, and coaches wait anxiously to see if it will be caught.

As exciting as it is, the long, deep pass has a much lower percentage of completion than all other forms of the forward pass. Yet when it works, it gains large chunks of yardage. But as any football fan knows, the long pass is accompanied by a lot of anticipation and anxiety as everyone waits for the ball to drop into the hands of the receiver who is streaking down the field. What a thrill if the ball is caught!

Nearly every athlete who comes to BYU is a gospel passer or a gospel receiver. Sometimes he is both. Many times the gospel passes are short, direct, and, most importantly, caught. But often they are dropped. Sometimes they are overthrown or underthrown, and sometimes the gospel passer is not really prepared to throw the gospel pass, resulting in an incomplete pass. But, oh, what a thrill to see that long, deep gospel pass being thrown by a good passer when it lands in the hands of the gospel receiver who tucks the ball into his heart and sprints into the waters of baptism.

* * *

In this story, the names have been changed because the long gospel pass is still in the air. I am anxiously praying that the ball will find its mark.

In the early part of June, 1989, the following letter arrived at my office in the equipment room of the George Albert Smith Fieldhouse:

> Dear Floyd,
> My name is Debbie Small. I am married to Jim Small. Jim wrestled for BYU in the 1960s. I hope you remember him.
> Jim and I have been married since 1965. I'm writing to ask for your help. Jim's heart is deeply troubled regarding his sins of some 20 years ago. His health is in serious jeopardy because of a drinking problem. Though Jim has never joined the Church, I have begged him to receive a priesthood blessing. He will not, except from one person. He will accept a priesthood blessing from you. He also desires to talk to you. With tears in his eyes, he has told me how much he loves you. He remembers with affection how long and hard you argued religion with him. Because of you, he has a respect for the members of the Church.
> I ask that you pray for Jim to find the courage to confess his sins and ask for God's help. You are very important to him, and I pray you will seek the direction of the Holy Ghost for Jim's benefit.
> We are planning a trip to Utah at the end of June for my 25th reunion. Jim will want to see you at that time if I cannot get him to come sooner.

Please fast and pray for Jim. Thank you for caring
for him so long ago. I'm concerned for Jim's soul and
for his happiness. I cling to the hope that he will talk
to you and put his life in order.
Thanks for your prayers.
Debbie

By the time I finished reading that letter, a thousand
memories of my experiences with Jim Small had been awak-
ened. Jim had come to BYU early in 1960. He was on a
wrestling scholarship, and part of that scholarship was in the
form of a grant-in-aid. That meant he could work for the
athletic department, earning a whopping $15 per month, or
$135 per year. Fifteen dollars in that day went a lot further
than it does now, and most of the scholarship kids funded their
dating through the grant-in-aid.

Jim's job was to work for me folding towels. We did most
of our folding in the mornings, and that was when Jim was in
his most argumentative mood. I've never figured out yet if
Jim was anti-religious or merely anti-agreeable. Our arguments were always about religion. We spoke in loud, obnox-
ious voices, and, yet, there was usually a feeling of camraderie
that made us both feel good about each other when we
finished working.

Sometimes Jim's arguments were so ridiculous I would
have to turn my head so he wouldn't see me smiling at him.
For the four years Jim was at BYU, we worked and argued—
cats and dogs couldn't have fought any better.

At the end of his junior year in school, Jim married Debbie,
and they had a baby girl before graduation. Jim asked that I
bless the baby and give her a special blessing.

In June of 1967, Jim graduated and took his family to
Southern California to teach in a junior high school. For all
I knew, he had dropped off the end of the earth. I didn't hear
a word from them until Debbie's letter arrived.

It was June 30, 1989, when Jim Small came walking into
the equipment room in the Fieldhouse. Even though I hadn't

seen him for more than 20 years, I recognized him immediately because he had changed so little physically. There were a few streaks of grey in his brown hair and a sign of aging wrinkles on a leathery face. But it was the same voice, the same careless manner.

Jim was carrying a large, wrapped package, which he handed to me. It was a picture of a rundown farm building he had painted only two days before. He had added snow on the ground so it would fit Utah's landscape. I had not known that Jim was an artist.

We talked for some time about his work and his family. We reminisced about our good times (arguments) when he was a student at BYU. Then, sensing that this conversation was going to need privacy, I suggested we go to the Marriott Center where we could get lost and talk our hearts out.

After we made our way into the basement of the Marriott Center, we sat down in a small office. I asked Jim if he had any questions. "Yes," he said, "I've come 700 miles to ask you two questions."

I looked at him for a moment and said, "Ask."

His first question took me by surprise. "Do you believe in the Immaculate Conception?"

"That's a Catholic term," I said. "We don't call it that. But if you are asking if we believe that Mary was the mother of Jesus and that Heavenly Father was the father of Jesus, yes, we believe that."

"I can't accept that," he snapped.

"Okay, then what's your second question?"

"If Jesus is the Savior of the whole world, as you tell me, why doesn't He appear to the Hindus and the Moslems?" Jim asked. "And why doesn't he appear to the American Indian?"

"Well," I said, "the appearance of the Savior to people is based on faith. If you don't believe in Him, you can't have much faith, and the Hindus don't accept him as the Savior, nor do the Moslems. As far as the American Indian is concerned, read this."

I tossed him a *Book of Mormon*. "That tells all about His appearance to the American Indians," I stated.

I didn't even bring up the Immaculate Conception doctrine again. For nearly two hours we talked, hidden away in the equipment room of the Marriott Center. As we were finishing our conversation, Jim asked me, "What time is your church on Sunday?"

"It's at 3:00," I said.

"Where do you meet?"

"In the old chapel across from the stadium. And it will be Fast Sunday."

He looked around the room and then at me. "Can I come?" he asked.

I assured him that he would be welcome. And I prayed from that moment until Sunday that the students in that ward would want to bear their testimonies so he would have a special experience.

I saw Debbie and Jim enter the chapel exactly at three o'clock, just as we were getting started. They sat down on the back row. The ward members didn't even know they were there. The meeting ran overtime because the kids stood up one after the other to bear their testimonies.

After the service was over, I made my way through the crowd to Jim and asked if he and Debbie would meet with me in my office. We visited for a few minutes before I finally turned to Jim and said, "I want to talk to you. And I want you to be quiet. I don't want any arguing. I want to talk, and I want you to listen."

Then I began to tell him about Jesus. "I didn't say too much about the Immaculate Conception," I reminded him. "You said you couldn't believe it, and that really doesn't bother me. There are so many other things that you have to believe first that the doctrine of Immaculate Conception will come automatically to you. Once you believe that Jesus is the Savior of the world, and once you can understand the importance of the Prophet Joseph Smith, all the other questions that you are asking will be answered. You have a tendency to pick out certain points in the gospel that bother you. But you've got to start with the basics. And then you've got to go through a process of repentance. Then, after all that, we can talk about baptism, and you can receive the Holy Ghost to be your help and your guide.

"Jim," I continued, "look back on your life. You have three daughters. What have you done to bless their lives? Think about that. What have you done spiritually in your family to bless the lives of your children and your wife? Have you prayed with them, gone to church with them? You are the patriarch of the family. Just think back and tell me what you have done."

I continued. "I'm sure you have done things for them physically—bringing home the bacon and things they needed. But how about emotional stability—those things that come from good faith and good understanding of our purpose here upon this earth? You don't even believe those concepts. How can you bless your family with something that is stable when you are not stable yourself?"

I talked about a lot of other ideas with Jim; then I said, "I want to give you a challenge. I want you to begin doing the things that you should have been doing a long, long time ago. I want you to be studying the scriptures. I want you to read the *Book of Mormon*. I want you to be praying with your family. Admittedly, you're unhappy."

He nodded and agreed that he was unhappy. We talked a little bit about his unhappiness, and then I said to him, "Jim, there is one other thing I want to do. I want to lay my hands on your head and give you a blessing."

He looked across the desk at me, then pointed his finger at me. "You, and no one else," he said.

"Me, and no one else except the Spirit of our Heavenly Father, which I am going to ask to be here to witness this blessing" I assured him.

I went behind him and laid my hands on his head and gave him a blessing. Before the blessing was through, I could hear him sniffing a little bit. I knew there were a few tears, and Debbie was also crying a little. When I finished, he stood up and we embraced.

We stood there for a few minutes chatting, because I had been pretty rough on him, and I wanted him to know I was his friend. I wasn't trying to destroy him. I was trying to wake him to spiritual things.

I told Jim I would send him a copy of *A Marvelous Work and a Wonder* and asked him to call or write me if he had any questions. A week later, I sent the book and a letter. I didn't hear anything from them after several months, so I sent another letter just to let them know I was thinking about them and that I loved them and was praying for them.

I still have not heard from Jim, but I am confident that one day I'm going to get a letter from him, and he is going to ask me to come to Santa Barbara to baptize him.

Now it's not important that *I* baptize Jim. The important thing is that he be baptized. I'm just waiting now for news to come from him. I don't know how long it's going to take, but it certainly is going to happen. I just don't know how long the ball is going to be in the air.

* * *

I witnessed a similar situation many years ago, although not with a BYU athlete. I was bishop in south Orem. Two motels were inside the boundaries of our ward. One was called the "Hacienda" and the other was the "Hillcrest."

Those motels usually attracted people who were just there for the weekend. So every Saturday evening, I would go to the Hacienda to see who was there. On one particular Saturday, I asked the landlady if she had any guests who would be staying for the weekend. She said there was a family in apartment No. 3 from Ohio, but she didn't know how long they were going to be staying.

I knocked on the door, and a big, stout man answered it. I introduced myself as Bishop Johnson of the Latter-day Saint Church in Orem.

He turned around and yelled, "Mabel, you've got some bishop out here who wants to talk to you!"

Mabel was a small woman. She and her husband, Jack, had two children with them. When she came to the door, I told her who I was. I mentioned that since the family was going to be in town on Sunday, I would like to invite them to come to church meetings the following day. "We have Sunday School at 10 a.m. and Sacrament Meeting at 3:30 in the afternoon," I said.

I found out that they were from Cincinnati and had been through Provo five years previously. On that initial trip, their car had broken down by the hospital in Provo on a Sunday. As they were standing around, wondering what they were going to do, a man in a pickup truck pulled up behind them and wanted to know if he could help them. They told him their car had quit working, and they didn't know what to do.

"I have a big house," he said, "Why don't I take you there?"

He drove them to his home and called a friend to tow the broken car to his garage so he could fix it. The next day the car was fixed, and the Good Samaritan sent the family on their way to California.

They returned to Cincinnati and noticed many of the problems of the big city, the most obvious of which was the racial unrest so prevalent at that time. One day Jack came home from work and said to Mabel, "I don't like all the tension and hostility here. I think it will only get worse. Let's sell out."

So they sold everything and headed west. Because of their previous good experience in Provo, they decided to spend a few days there.

That's when I showed up at their motel door.

The next day they came to Sunday School and to Sacrament Meeting. I introduced them to the Relief Society and Primary presidents. Mabel attended Relief Society on Tuesday and the kids went to Primary on Wednesday. Then they came back again to meetings the following Sunday. Within three weeks we had the stake missionaries teaching them. And within four weeks Mabel and the two boys were baptized into the church.

But Jack didn't want to join.

I took him to ballgames in the Smith Fieldhouse, and I took him to the welfare farm to pick apples. He couldn't understand why a church would have a fruit farm. So I took him to the Bishop's Storehouse. Finally, he was impressed.

The family lived here nearly three months before he got a job in the northwest.

Ten years later, I received a letter from some missionaries in Seattle, who said there was a man up there named Jack McGee who was a scout master and an assistant to the president of the Sunday School, but he wasn't a member of the Church. They had challenged him to be baptized, and he agreed on one condition: that Bishop Johnson come to Seattle to baptize him. I think he said that because he didn't think I would go all the way to Seattle for a baptism.

The missionaries had set the date for September 17. That happened to be a weekend when the BYU football team was going out of town, so I told the coaches I wasn't going to be traveling with them. I was driving to Seattle. The missionaries wrote me to say that everything was set up—the baptism would take place on Saturday.

My wife, a couple of my Indian children, and two members of my ward drove with me all the way to Seattle and found the chapel. When we got there, we saw that the entire ward was in attendance. There must have been 300 people at Jack's baptism. I baptized him and I confirmed him. Then the next day we stayed overnight and attended church with him and his family. During the meeting, Jack stood and gave a beautiful testimony.

I kept in touch with the McGees over the years. They moved to California, and I went to dinner with them when BYU played in the Freedom Bowl. As we were sitting at the table, Jack looked at me and said, "You sure got me into a pack of trouble."

"I did?"

"Yeah, do you know what they have me doing now? I'm the High Priest group leader. And all those guys want to do is sleep. If you hadn't been messing around visiting that motel in Orem, I would have never had this problem."

Mabel looked over and said, "Jack, why don't you tell him the truth? Why don't you tell him you're the happiest you have ever been in your life and that you wouldn't trade your calling as High Priest group leader for any job in the church?"

Jack looked at me, and then he looked at Mabel. Then he said, "Honey, I wouldn't tell him that because it would make him so happy he couldn't stand it."

That gospel pass was in the air for 10 years. It took a lot of patience to wait and see if Jack was going to run under it and catch it. He finally did, and his family will be forever grateful.

* * *

Tommy Holmoe was an All-WAC defensive back for us in the early 1980s. He was a bright young man and an outstanding football player. I often wondered why he was never baptized.

He married a BYU cheerleader from California. She was LDS but couldn't convince Tom to join the Church. After leaving BYU, Tom was drafted by the San Francisco 49ers in 1983 and made the team as a safety. The 49ers were my favorite team back then, and they still are, so I watch them whenever they play on Monday Night Football.

In February, 1987, I was in the Marriott Center preparing the uniforms for a game the next night. About 4 o'clock a knock came on the equipment room door. I knew it wasn't somebody who had been there before because people don't usually knock. They just plow right in. I opened the door, and there stood Tom Holmoe.

"Tom, what are you doing here?" I asked.

"My wife and I came up to see her parents who live here now," he explained.

I invited him in, and we talked about Steve Young, Todd Shell, and Bill Ring, former BYU athletes then playing with the 49ers.

Finally I said, "You must have a real purpose for coming here. Can I help you in any way?"

"Yes," he said.

I wasted no time. "How come you haven't been baptized into the Church yet?" I asked.

"That's what I came here to talk to you about. I didn't come to Provo to be baptized, but I was driving around the BYU campus, and I got the impression that now is the time that I should be baptized. I don't know what to do about it, and I knew you would, so I've been looking for you for the last couple of hours. I want to find out what I need to do to be baptized."

That's about the easiest question I've ever been asked.

"I'm going to call the full-time missionaries," I told him. "If you will give me the phone number where I can reach you here in Provo, I'll have the missionaries call you. When are you going back to San Francisco?"

"Monday."

"Today's Wednesday. That means you'll be baptized Saturday. I'll have the full-time missionaries call you and interview you so they can set a baptismal date. Have you had the missionary lessons?"

He said he had taken them several years before.

"Any questions you need to ask me?" I inquired.

"No, I have been doing a lot of thinking these past 24 hours, and a lot of things are coming back to me about the missionary discussions."

I called Tom later that night, but the missionaries still hadn't reached him. So I called the missionaries, and they said, "We thought maybe we'd phone him tomorrow."

"No you're not," I said. "You call him now. He has come all this way to be baptized, and we're going to baptize him."

They called Tom that night. The next night Tom phoned me to say the service would be at 11:00 on Saturday. I was there and it was a beautiful service. Tom was baptized by his father-in-law. Then as Tom bore his testimony, I sat there trying to hold back the tears, while listening to him talk about his faith in the Lord and his faith in the Church and of his experience of coming here and having the spirit whisper that he should be baptized.

He came back last March to help with spring football practice. We talked more about his conversion. He is an outstanding young man. The gospel pass thrown to Tom was in the air for five years. The good defensive back that he is, he intercepted it and headed for the end zone!

3

Redshirt or Whiteshirt?

I firmly believe that Brigham Young University has a mandate. The coaches say it is to win championships. But since BYU is a church university, I strongly feel that its primary mission is to teach the gospel. Every department on campus has that mandate.

I have a cousin named Janie Thompson who helped establish the Program Bureau years ago. She feels the same way I do about BYU's mission. In all the trips she's made—in particular with the Lamanite Generation—the primary objective was to leave some kind of impression or testimony wherever they went. They obviously succeeded because many of the new doors opening for the Church around the world were jarred loose by these wonderful BYU entertainers.

Our athletic teams can, and should, have the same priority. I realize not everyone at BYU feels the same as I do on that point, but I am convinced the Lord feels that way. Our athletic teams must deliver a message to the people of the world. We can do it by winning. We can do it by losing. It is us—we, ourselves—who fulfill that mandate.

Many of the young athletes who come to BYU catch the missionary spirit. They have heard the prophets speak about the importance of serving a mission, and they want to be part of that exciting work. However, they often are torn between serving a full-time mission and using their athletic talents here at BYU. They realize that they will be walking away from the glory and fame heaped upon successful athletes if they decide to accept a mission call. They also know they might lose their competitive edge while preaching the gospel and never return to their pre-mission form. These wonderful young men spend many agonizing hours mulling over the options: redshirt or whiteshirt?

Up until the early 1970s, The Decision was made easier by the fact that most of the coaches discouraged their athletes from going into the mission field. They believed mission life would soften their athletes and make them lose their aggressiveness. Opponents often said BYU would never be competitive in football because of the missionary program.

But when the school named LaVell Edwards head football coach, he was much more receptive to the mission idea. He told his players they were free to serve missions if they decided to do so. As a result, more and more football players began leaving on missions.

They continued to return fat and out of shape, but Coach Edwards discovered that they were more mature. They were more disciplined. *Life* for these young men was more important than football. Before long, opposing coaches began complaining about the "advantage" BYU was receiving from the missionary program.

Even with all the success BYU's football program reaped from the missionary system, BYU's basketball players rarely served missions. It was assumed basketball players would have a harder time returning to pre-mission form than football players. Then Devin Durrant went to Spain on a mission and returned two years later to become an All-American. Devin's post-mission success seemed to encourage other players. Since 1983, nearly every LDS basketball player has gone on a mission.

In spite of the increased popularity of serving missions, many of the athletes still struggle with The Decision. They have visions of a pro career. Or they are afraid their beautiful girlfriend will not be here when they get back.

* * *

One athlete who had a particularly difficult struggle with The Decision was Vai Sikahema, a football player from Arizona. Originally, Vai and his whole family were from Tonga. The father moved them to Mesa so they could attend school. Vai was a highly recruited athlete and eventually came to BYU.

When I first looked at Vai, I wondered what he had that was going to make him a football player because it certainly wasn't his size. He was only about 5 feet 9 inches tall and weighed maybe 180 pounds. But what he lacked in size, he made up for in speed and determination. He was committed to becoming a good running back. But his real skill was as a kick return specialist.

During his freshman year (the fall of 1980), Vai came to see me in mid-October. He said something was bothering him. I asked what it was, and he said, "I made my mind up a long time ago that I didn't want to go on a mission. But something is always eating at me, telling me I should go. But I don't want to go!"

I said, "Well, you've made your mind up that you don't want to go on a mission, so you shouldn't worry about it anymore."

Two weeks later, he was back in my office. He said, "Floyd, I don't want to go on a mission, but this feeling that I should go on a mission is bugging me."

Every two or three weeks thereafter, Vai would wander in and tell me the same thing.

BYU lost its first game that year to New Mexico but went on to win 11 straight games and the Western Athletic Conference championship. The Cougar offense, led by quarterback Jim McMahon, was perhaps the best ever in the history of college football. By winning the WAC, BYU was invited to play Southern Methodist in the Holiday Bowl. Every BYU sports fan knows about the miracle finish in that game. BYU came from three touchdowns behind in the closing minutes of the game to pull off a victory as time ran out.

Vai played a significant role in that victory. Shortly before the end of the first half, he returned a punt more than 80 yards for a touchdown. Then he stood in the endzone doing a Tongan war dance. Standing on the sidelines watching him, I thought, "Goodbye mission. Vai doesn't have to worry about that anymore. He'll never go on a mission now."

After the game, he went home to Mesa to spend Christmas with his family. When he returned to Provo in January, he walked into my office again and said, "I don't know what to do about this problem. I don't want to go on a mission, yet this thing is really bothering me."

"Well, Vai," I said, "Do you want to talk to one of the General Authorities?"

"Yea, man!" he said. "I'd like that."

"Would you like to talk to President Kimball?" I asked.

"No, I don't want to talk to him. I know what he'd tell me."

"Okay," I said. "Would you like to talk to Elder Paul Dunn?"

Vai was thrilled with that suggestion, so I asked if he wanted me to call Brother Dunn to set up the appointment or if he wanted to make the call himself. He suggested that I make the call, so I got on the phone and told Brother Dunn about Vai's problem. He asked what Vai really wanted to talk about. I told Brother Dunn that Vai wanted him to tell him whether or not he should go on a mission.

"I can't do that," Brother Dunn said.

I suggested he share some advice with Vai that I apparently was failing to offer. He agreed, and we set up an appointment for Vai to meet with him on February 24, 1981.

Vai met Elder Dunn at 5:00 or 5:30 in the evening. Later that night he came walking back into the equipment room.

"How did it go?" I asked.

"Wonderful!" he exclaimed.

"What did he tell you?"

Vai smiled and said, "He told me to go get my patriarchal blessing and do what it tells me to do. I'm going to see my bishop tonight so I can get a recommend."

A little more than a month passed before Vai brought his blessing in to show me. One portion of it stated that Vai would teach the gospel to his family.

"Well Vai," I smiled, "looks like you're going to Tonga."

He said, "It sure looks like it, doesn't it?"

"So you are going to go on a mission?" I questioned.

Vai nodded his head and said, "It says right here that I will teach the gospel to my family. So of course I'll go on a mission."

He got his mission call to Sioux Falls, South Dakota.

When he showed me his mission call, I asked, "Do you have any family in South Dakota?"

He assured me he knew of no relatives up there. "Are there any Tongans up there?" I asked. Again, he said he didn't know of any.

"That's really strange to be told you would teach the gospel to your family in your patriarchal blessing and then be sent clear out there on your mission," I commented.

Vai left late that spring to preach the gospel in Sioux Falls.

At about noon on a Saturday in June, the phone rang in my office. I was surprised to hear Vai Sikahema on the other end.

"Floyd," he said, "I've had the greatest thrill of my life. I just baptized my first family today, and I'll tell you there are no thrills on earth, including all the thrills in football, that will ever compare to being able to baptize somebody into the church.

"I feel ten feet tall today and I didn't know who I wanted to share this with, but your name came to mind, so I took a chance of calling you on the phone."

I was really pleased to hear he was having a great experience in the mission field. Then I remembered his patriarchal blessing.

"By the way," I said, "are there any Tongans out there?"

"Tongans?" he asked. "Why would there need to be any Tongans?"

"Oh, I don't know, except that your patriarchal blessing said you were going to teach the gospel to your family," I explained.

He laughed and said, "I'm teaching the gospel to the Lamanites. We're from the same lineage. They are my family."

It had not occurred to me that Vai would be teaching the Lamanites. But he was doing exactly what his patriarchal blessing said he would do.

Vai served a great mission. Twice after he was released, he went back to the mission field representing BYU. He travelled through North and South Dakota once under the sponsorship of the mission president. Then the school district there asked him to come back and hold clinics with the kids and teach them about sports and life.

In my opinion, Vai prepared himself for life by going on that mission. He did more missionary work, did it more effectively, and impressed more people than if he had stayed to play football at BYU.

And by the way, he did continue to play football for BYU when he returned home. He set an NCAA career punt-return record and was one of the best return specialists ever to play at BYU. The pro scouts noticed him too, and he was drafted by the St. Louis Cardinals of the NFL. In his first two seasons with the Cardinals, Vai was selected to play in the Pro Bowl, an honor given only to the very best players at each position.

But if you ask Vai, he will probably tell you he would rather be all-pro on the Lord's team than an NFL all-star.

* * *

I remember a young man from Denver who played football for BYU in the mid 1970s. His name was Clark Carlson. During the summer between his junior and senior seasons, Clark caught the mission bug and, without saying anything to anyone, sent in his papers and got his mission call.

When he came in and told me he was going to go to Southern California on a mission, I was totally surprised. Clark had one more year of eligibility left, and it was rather unusual for a young man to leave that late in his career.

"Have you talked to Coach Edwards yet?" I asked.

"No."

"I think you ought to go talk to him," I said. "I'm sure he is planning on you starting for the defense next year."

So Clark went in and spoke with Coach Edwards. Coach, naturally, was concerned about the timing of Clark's mission and asked him to delay leaving for four or five months. They called the missionary committee and received permission from them to wait until the end of the season. Everyone felt goodabout it. Clark returned to school and finished his eligibility that fall. He was scheduled to enter the missionary home on January 8, but I didn't see him until after classes began winter semester. He had a roommate named Blake Murdock, a returned missionary football player, who spent a lot of time working out in the George Albert Smith Fieldhouse.

I saw Blake about January 5 and asked him if Clark was ready to enter the mission home.

"He's not going now," Blake said.

"He's not going?" I asked, shocked.

"That's right. He got his call but changed his mind and decided he's not going."

"You listen to me," I told Blake. "You have that guy come up to the Marriott Center and see me at 3:00 this afternoon."

It was a Wednesday afternoon, and I didn't know if he was going to come or not. But I was working in the equipment room when Clark came walking in at 3:00.

"Well, are you ready to go into the mission home?" I asked, pretending not to know about his change of heart.

"No," he said. "I'm not going."

"Why aren't you going?" I probed. "You've already got your call."

He wouldn't tell me the real reason. (I found out later it was a girlfriend.) He just said, "I don't want to go."

"Clark," I said. "I want to talk to you for a minute. Sit down here."

He took a seat, and I pulled out my Bible and turned to the 21st chapter of Matthew. In that chapter, Jesus gives a parable. It begins with the words, "What think ye?"

"A certain man had two sons; and he came to the first and said, Son, go work today in my vineyard. He answered and said, I will not: but afterward repented, and went. And he came to the second, and said likewise. And he answered and said, I go, sir: and went not" (Matthew 21: 28-30).

In the next verse, the Savior asks which of the sons did the will of his father. The publicans and others to whom Jesus was speaking agreed that the first son had done the father's will, and the Savior told them they were right.

By this time, Clark was beginning to get my message. "You know," I continued, "when we do the will of our Heavenly Father, He says that everything He has will be ours. But when we don't do His will, we don't get anything.

"Now, for just a minute, I want you to think about which of these sons you are. Are you number one or number two?

Clark just sat there, real sober. He looked up at me and, with a sorrowful voice, said, "I guess I'm number two."

"And you're not doing the will of your Father," I added.

"But I turned my mission call back," he said, trying to find some sympathy and mercy from me.

"Who did you turn it in to?" I asked.

"My bishop."

"Go see your bishop and tell him you want that mission call back."

"Do you really think I could do it?" he asked.

"Sure," I said. "You go see your bishop. And don't waste any time because you've got to be in the mission home on Friday.

Clark shot out of that room like he was chasing after a quarterback. And when he came to see me Friday morning, he really looked bushed. He had to go find that mission call and get it back again. He had to get all the clothes he needed and get everything in order. He even had to call Denver to tell his parents he had changed his mind.

At 2:00 that Friday afternoon, Clark was in the mission home in Salt Lake City. As things turned out, he served a great mission and held some important leadership positions. Yes, he lost his girlfriend while he was gone. But he returned to BYU and married one of the most beautiful girls I have ever seen.

They live in Denver now and have a lovely little family. Every time he comes to Provo, Clark comes in to talk to me about his mission call and what it meant to him in his life.

* * *

We have had many athletes who didn't go into the mission field and yet turned out to be tremendous missionaries right here on campus and in the community. Two that come to mind are Orrin Olsen and Paul Linford. They played together in the early 1970s and both were outstanding athletes. Paul was a three-time All-WAC defensive tackle. Orrin also started his career on the defensive line but eventually earned all-conference honors playing center on offense.

Beginning with their freshmen years, those two kids had a nagging feeling they should go on missions. It was about November of their first year when both of them came in and wanted to talk.

"What are we going to talk about?" I asked.

Orrin was from Orem, and Paul was from Salt Lake City. They said they had gone home over the weekend, and their bishops had asked them to start thinking about a mission.

"We had already decided we probably wouldn't be going on missions," they said, "and their prodding got us a little bit upset. We wanted to know what you think about it."

"Well, missions are awfully important," I stated.

"But don't you think we can serve a mission here at BYU playing football?" they asked.

"I guess you can," I said. "But I don't know how well prepared you are to be missionaries or how effective you will be."

Orrin had two brothers, Merlin and Phil, who had played professional football. Neither of them had served missions. Paul's father was a stake president. Both Paul and Orrin had been presidents of their seminary classes their senior year in high school. They were outstanding young men in every way.

We talked for quite a while that day, and finally I said, "I think two guys with your athletic ability could serve well wherever you are. But I would really need to think about this for a while."

"Floyd," they said, "will you pray about whether we should go on a mission?"

"Why don't you pray about it yourselves?" I asked.

"We have," they said, "but we don't get an answer."

"What makes you feel if I pray I will get an answer?"

"You're closer to Him than we are," they insisted. "Won't you please pray about it?"

"Okay," I consented, "I'll pray about it."

That conversation took place on a Wednesday, and the next morning they came in about 7:00 and asked if I had prayed for them.

"Yea, I prayed about it."

"What did the Lord tell you?" they asked.

I shook my head. "I get the feeling that you think that all I have to do is open the door, and He's standing there so I can ask Him a question."

"Well, what did He tell you?" they inquired.

"I'm not sure He told me anything," I said.

"But you did pray, didn't you?"

"Yes, I told you I prayed."

"If you prayed He must have told you something."

I shook my head again. "Listen. I got a feeling. I'm just afraid to tell you what it is."

"What was it?" they quizzed.

"I really feel that some day you guys are going to serve missions," I stated. "But for right now the Lord would like you to use your athletic ability to teach the gospel to the young people around here."

They stared at me for a minute but didn't seem impressed. I felt I had taken a real chance saying something like that because everyone knew I was so pro-mission.

Later that afternoon, they stopped by the equipment room before practice to tell me that they had an appointment the next day to see Elder Paul Dunn.

"What are you going to see him for?" I asked.

"We're going to ask him the same questions we asked you."

"Wait a minute," I said, "Don't put my word against Brother Dunn's to see who is going to get the most inspiration on this thing."

But they went to see him anyway, and I didn't see them again until the following Monday. They came walking in bright and early with smiles on their faces.

"We had a great time last Friday up in Salt Lake City," they said. "We talked to Elder Dunn for nearly 45 minutes."

"What did he tell you?" I asked, worried that he might have given them exactly the opposite counsel I had given.

"He told us about his experience in pro baseball and how the crusty old managers used to come into his room in the middle of the night to ask him questions about why he was like he was."

"That's nice," I said, "but what did he *tell* you?"

"He told us about his experience in World War II and how he had the opportunity to share his testimony with his buddies on the front line."

"Okay," I said, growing a little restless. "But what did he *tell* you?"

"He told us about his experiences travelling throughout the church and meeting the young people and how much faith he had in them."

Then right in the middle of a sentence, one of them stopped and said, "Do you know what he told us?"

"No," I said. "What did he tell you?"

"He told us that we should use our athletic ability and our talents to teach the gospel. And in every game we play, we ought to choose someone from the other team and ask him the Golden Question."

I never would have thought of that.

This was back in the days when freshmen couldn't play varsity ball, and BYU had a freshman football team. Our next game was against the Air Force Academy.

"So you're going to ask the Golden Question to one of the players from the Air Force Academy?"

"Yes, sir," they said, "that's our plan."

I was really curious about how they would pull off their pigskin proselyting. But they insisted they would do as Nephi had done and trust in the Lord to find a way for them to accomplish His work. They were very serious about their assignment and came in often to cook up their scheme to corner an Air Force cadet long enough to ask him the Golden Question.

Their initial plan was to walk around the Academy and pick out the scrawniest guy they could find and then back him into a corner and ask him the Golden Question. That would have been easy because Paul weighed 260 pounds and Orrin weighed 240. Both played on the defensive line their freshman year.

"But I thought it was supposed to be a football player," I reminded them.

So they next decided they would stand in front of the Air Force Academy dressing room, waiting for a likely candidate to walk by. Then they would grab him, pull him around the corner, and ask him the Golden Question.

Well, that plan didn't work either because our football coaches knew nothing of the scheme and didn't let the players out before the game. So all during the first half of that game, Paul and Orrin were wondering how they could get an Air Force football player in a situation to ask him about the Church.

At halftime, during the chalk talk, those two guys were in the corner looking at a game program, studying each name number by number, trying to get some sort of inspiration about who they were going to ask the Golden Question. But they didn't get any inspiration.

In the middle of the third quarter, BYU's defense had just come off the field. One of them approached the other and said, "I know who it's going to be."

"Who?" asked the other.

"The quarterback. He only weighs 175 pounds, and we're going to get him and ask him the Golden Question."

"How are we going to do that?" he asked.

"When we go back out on that field, they are going to try to run the football, and we're not going to let them do it so they have to pass on third down. That's when you and I are going to sack the quarterback. The guy who gets him down first will ask the Golden Question."

They were so excited about their plan that they hoped BYU would fumble so they could get back out there on the field.

They must have had strong faith because the Cougars did fumble, and those two missionaries—all 500 pounds of them—ran out onto the field. Air Force went into its offensive huddle, and BYU was in its defensive huddle. Orrin and Paul were patting each other on the seat of their pants, anxious to do some "laying on of hands."

In two downs, the Air Force Academy made only 2 yards. It was third and eight yards to go for a first down—a likely passing situation. When the quarterback got the ball, he stepped back into the pocket to try to find someone open for a pass. No one was clear, so he shifted to the other side of the pocket.

But he didn't make it.

Paul, the big defensive tackle, picked him up, threw him to the ground, and fell on top of him. No sooner had Paul pinned him to the ground than Orrin fell right on top of them.

Think of it. There were 500 pounds of priesthood on that little old quarterback. Paul looked down through the facemask into the quarterback's eyes, which appeared as if they were going to pop right out of their sockets, and said to him in the best missionary voice he had ever used, "What do you know about the Mormon Church?"

That little quarterback kind of blinked his eyes and shook his head a little, trying to clear his mind. And finally he said, in a squeaky voice, "Plenty. Get off me. I'm a Mormon!"

Those two athletes were great missionaries. I can't tell you how many hundreds of young people sat at their feet and listened to them share their testimony of the gospel, or how many times I knelt in prayer with them.

Before every game, Paul and I would go upstairs in the Fieldhouse and have a word of prayer together to quiet him down so he could go out and play football.

* * *

All the stories of athletes serving missions don't have fairy tale endings. It's true that some promising athletes go into the mission field and, when they return, never pick up where they left off. There are various reasons for this. Sometimes they develop health problems during their missions. Often their perspectives change, and they simply don't care to play in competitive athletics anymore. Some want to give their full time to studies. And there are cases where the players recruited to take their places are better athletes.

I think of Bob Jensen, a quarterback on the football team. Bob had a difficult time making up his mind about going on a mission, but he finally decided to go. When he returned, he had some disappointing years in football. Yet if you were to talk to Bob Jensen today, he would tell you that one of the greatest things he ever did—next to marrying Debbie—was to serve the Lord as a missionary.

Steve Lindsley, another quarterback, will tell you the same thing about his mission experience. He, like Bob, sacrificed his athletic career to be part of the missionary force. Many others have suffered the same fate, but they never regret their decision to be missionaries.

Those who choose to "whiteshirt" might not set any NCAA records when they return to school, but they have accomplished much more than that. They have stored up treasures in heaven, which will last for the eternities.

Fourth and Long

For more than 30 years, I have met nearly every athlete who has participated in athletics at BYU. I have rubbed shoulders with future Hall of Famers. I have washed the uniforms of future millionaires. I have counseled all-stars-to-be about everything from missions to marriage.

But the most inspirational part of my job is not watching those who come here with a lot of notoriety, but rather observing the boy or girl who comes to BYU lacking physical skills possessed by others but exhibiting a strong desire to achieve. They have a message to share, a mission to achieve. There have been hundreds of them over the years. They don't care that the odds are stacked against them. They don't care that they supposedly don't have the physical ability to succeed in major-college sports. They don't care that the coaches have not considered their talent sufficient to warrant a scholarship.

These young men believe in themselves. They know they can succeed. For them, every down is fourth down and long. But they will never punt. They defy the odds and push on toward life's end zone.

* * *

When Chuck Cutler graduated from Alta High School in Salt Lake City, he was an all-state football player. He played for one year at Snow Junior College in Ephraim, Utah, and then decided to serve a mission. When he returned, football was still in his blood, and he decided to try for a spot on the Cougar roster.

One of the things that urged Chuck on was the belief that he could play major-college football; he believed in himself.

Chuck heard about the BYU Speakers' Bureau and the athletes who went out to speak to young people throughout the community: the Steve Youngs, the Trevor Matiches, the Todd Shells. Those athletes had gone out to share their testimonies. He thought that was a wonderful thing for an athlete to do. And deep in his heart, he wanted to succeed enough that the kids would recognize him and listen to what he had to say when he went out to share his testimony.

So when he got to BYU, he went to see Norm Chow, coach of the wide receivers. Coach Chow remembered Chuck from his Snow College playing days. He knew Chuck had decent speed—although it was not blazing—so Coach Chow told him to come down to the equipment room and check out a pair of shoes and report to practice that afternoon. Chuck came back to the equipment room and told the assistant equipment manager that Coach Chow had sent him to get some shoes.

The assistant told him, "You'll never make it on the football team. I'm not going to give you a pair of shoes."

Chuck didn't argue. He just went back up to Coach Chow and told him the equipment room wouldn't check him out any shoes. He then told the coach he was on his way to buy a pair of his own.

"No you're not," Coach Chow said, and he got on the phone to the equipment room and instructed the assistant to check him out a pair of shoes.

"You can't believe the shoes they gave me," Chuck said. "They weren't only worn out. They were worn in and around and everything else. But I put on those shoes and went to practice."

Later that year, Coach Edwards called Chuck into his office and told him that he would be put on scholarship. That was during his sophomore year.

One of the assistant linebacker coaches later came up to him and said, "Cutler, the biggest mistake this university has made up to now is putting you on scholarship. You'll never make it."

"That really made me feel wonderful to think that all those people had so much faith in me, but I believed in myself and I believed I had a message," Cutler told me.

"The Apostle Paul wrote a letter to Timothy in which he said, 'Stir up the gift of God that is within you.' (2 Timothy 1:6) And then he wrote another letter to the Philippians and said, 'I can do all things through Christ which strengtheneth me.' (Philippians 4:13)

"I decided that I was going to succeed because I had something that I needed to do," Chuck said. "I had a message I wanted to give. I could only prepare myself through football to fulfill the dream that I had within my heart.

"Chuck," I asked while he was telling me this story, "how many operations have you gone through?"

"I've gone through seven operations on my hand and one on my ankle," he replied.

"Didn't you ever get the message that maybe football wasn't your sport?"

"It never even entered my mind. Paul said, 'You stirred up the gift of God that is within you.' And I felt I had that spirit within me. It just needed to be stirred up. I was going to succeed. I had a message that I wanted to give, and I had to use football as a medium to give that message. So I never did worry about the operations. I had a deep desire grow within me to fulfill that dream. Consequently, this year has, perhaps, been the greatest year of my life as far as doing the thing that I really came here to do. I have no desire to play professional football. I just had a message to give the young people, and I got the opportunity to deliver it."

Chuck Cutler set some amazing records at BYU. But the most amazing statistic of all is that 43 times during his senior year, he had the opportunity to speak in public and share his testimony with young people. How many thousands came under the influence of his testimony we will never know. I imagine many of them have become better boys and girls and better men and women and have created goals within their hearts to achieve because of his words and counsel.

Chuck Cutler was both all-conference and academic All-American. He is a real example of what success is and how athletics can be used to touch the hearts of young people.

* * *

In the fall of 1980, we had an athlete come here from Greenwich, Connecticut. His name was Steve Young, and he played quarterback. He was left-handed, and we hadn't had a lot of southpaws play quarterback here.

Steve was an outstanding athlete, but his only drawback was that his high school didn't play football like it is played at BYU. They ran the wishbone, which meant either Steve handed the ball to a running back, or he ran the ball himself. He was fast, but because of his lack of experience throwing the football, he didn't seem to fit the mold of a BYU quarterback. He wasn't overly encouraged when the coaches listed him at the bottom of the depth chart at the quarterback position and then suggested he switch from quarterback to defensive back. Steve had a tremendous desire to play quarterback, and he became very discouraged about his prospects of playing anywhere but that position. Then one weekend the quarterback coach told him to show up at practice the following Monday wearing a white jersey, which meant he would be playing defense.

In a moment of depression, Steve called his dad and told him the coaches wanted him to play defense. Steve told his father that he wasn't too keen about that idea. In fact, he announced that he was going to quit and return home rather than stoop to playing defense.

That phone call changed Steve's life.

His dad, who had played football at BYU himself and earned the nickname "Grit," asked Steve to repeat what he had just said. Steve said he was going to quit football and return home.

"Steve, I only want to repeat this once, and I want you to listen," Grit said in his grittiest voice. "You have your free agency to quit football, and I'm not going to interfere with your free agency. But I'll tell you this: If you quit football, you can't come home because I don't want a quitter in the family."

Then the phone went dead.

That next Monday when Steve went out onto the field for practice, he was wearing his blue practice jersey. He ignored the coach's order and continued working out with the quarterbacks as if nothing had been said about switching to defense.

There is no need to rehash what happened to Steve Young. He enjoyed one of the most productive careers in collegiate football history. He set many NCAA records. He was runner-up in balloting for the Heisman Trophy. He signed what was at that time the most lucrative contract in professional sports—as a quarterback.

All that came about because Steve Young stirred up the gift of God that was in him. It doesn't make any difference whether he is running or passing or what he is doing; Steve Young is an All-American not only in the hearts of those who love athletics but also in the hearts of all those who know him.

* * *

J ason Buck is another good example of someone who did not believe his detractors and followed his dreams to greatness. He claimed St. Anthony, Idaho, as home, but he grew up in various Idaho communities. The Bucks were a very poor family, and Jason's clothes reflected their poverty. His pants had holes in the knees, and he owned just a couple of T-shirts to wear all year. After one move, the family spent the summer sleeping under an old truck, using bags of wheat as pillows. Finally, the family gathered enough scrap lumber from a condemned railroad depot to build a house.

The family's poverty, combined with the fact that they were Mormon, made Jason a target for cruel jokes and taunts from his classmates. Jason responded to the unkindness by thrashing his tormentors until he became known as the neighborhood bully.

Jason's one motivation in life was to play professional football. He declared that goal when, as a seven-year-old, he walked into the family room and saw his father and brother watching a professional football game on TV. "I'm going to play football someday," he vowed.

Such statements, repeated in public, only gave more ammunition to his detractors. But Jason believed in himself—he stirred up the gift of God that was within him. He became a starting quarterback as a freshman at Adrian High School and later moved to St. Anthony, where he beat out the starting quarterback for the job. Jason's teammates didn't welcome the new kid on the block with open arms. In fact, they resented having an upstart from Adrian push aside their buddy who had been quarterback the year before. At times the offensive linemen purposefully would not block the defenders, so Jason would be smashed to the ground.

Jason was an adequate high school quarterback, but his play did not cause any excitement among college recruiters. Most observers admitted Jason's football career was over when he finally graduated from high school. But Jason had other ideas.

He went to Ricks College, only a short drive from St. Anthony, and asked to try out for the team. By that time, he was about 6-foot-5 and weighed maybe 200 pounds. The coaches timed him at 4.6 in the 40-yard-dash, which is pretty fast, even for a running back. "You have the potential to play pro football as a defensive lineman," one coach told him. They liked him—but not enough to give him a scholarship.

Without a grant-in-aid, Jason couldn't afford to stay in school, so he quit and went back to St. Anthony, where he learned his parents were getting a divorce.

Most people would have given up on their dream after such experiences. But Jason was more determined than ever. He picked up odd jobs building fences, stacking 100-pound bags of seed, and stocking shelves in a supermarket. After a hard day's work, he would head for the weight room to develop his already tired muscles.

The routine continued for two years. And by that time, everyone but Jason had forgotten The Dream. But the hard work hefting seed sacks and lifting weights had added 30 pounds of muscle to Jason's frame, and he returned to Ricks one last time in pursuit of a football career.

This time the coaches noticed the new-and-improved Jason Buck. They were no dummies. He had the size, the speed, and the determination that only the great players possess. So they gave him a scholarship, and he wasn't long in rewarding their generosity. He had 17 quarterback sacks his freshman year and a national-record 25 his sophomore year. One magazine named him its national defensive player-of-the-year. And college recruiters were beating a path to Rexburg,

Idaho, to see how this young man had bucked the odds. Suddenly, those people who had laughed at his dream were not snickering so loudly.

Jason and his new wife, Roxi, elected to attend BYU and they moved to Provo. Despite the football accolades, Jason's and Roxi's finances hadn't improved any. Their student apartment had no furniture when they first arrived in Provo. They ate and slept on the floor and struggled to make ends meet.

However, it wasn't long before Jason showed he was a legitimate pro prospect. He was named all-conference after his junior year and repeated as a senior. The football writers around the country voted him the recipient of the Outland Trophy, given to the outstanding lineman in college football each year. It was only the third time in the history of the award that a player from the West had won. The next year he was a first-round draft choice of the Cincinnati Bengals and played in the Super Bowl two years later. Jason defied the odds. He had stirred up the gift of God inside him and chased his dream. He had gone from a poor, gangly bully to an idolized pro football star.

Jason shared his story with hundreds of young people. He showed them by his own example what could be accomplished with the help of God and a never-say-die attitude. He knocked down each obstacle and created from it a stepping stone to higher goals and dreams.

* * *

Not all of BYU's great athletes are football or basketball players. There was a wrestler at BYU named Rhondo Fehlberg. He was the second of five brothers who came to BYU. Rhondo was one of the first BYU wrestlers to achieve national ranking. One year he qualified for the NCAA championships in Maryland. He advanced to the second round of the tournament but suffered a serious injury in that match. The trainers determined he had torn the ligaments in his knee.

Any other wrestler probably would have thrown in the towel and gone home. The situation looked extremely bleak for Rhondo. But he hadn't gone to Maryland simply to turn around and fly home without finishing. So he got the trainer at the University of Maryland to fix him up as best he could and get him back onto the mat. He not only continued wrestling, but he also captured fifth place in the tournament an impressive feat for a healthy person.

Rhondo had a goal and a message. And, like the other athletes I've mentioned in this chapter, he wasn't going to let anything prevent him from reaching that goal.

After his senior year, Rhondo decided to go into the mission field. The summer before he left, he worked for a friend, a contractor who agreed to fund his mission. But three or four months after he had left for the mission field, Rhondo's friend filed for bankruptcy and had to withdraw his support.

I became concerned about whether Rhondo was going to be able to stay on his mission. I had some friends who had money, so I contacted them and arranged for them to join me in donating a little each month to keep Rhondo on his mission. He had a girlfriend, Mary, and I thought I ought to let her know of our plans to help out.

One day I saw her jogging on the track. I stopped her and said, "Mary, I hear Rhondo has been having some financial troubles, and I want you to know that I have those problems all solved. I have a few men who are going to contribute about $50 per month, and we'll be able to send him $200 a month."

She looked at me and put her hands on her hips and said, "Who told you to do that?"

"No one told me to do that," I said. "In this life you're supposed to have yourself organized. The Lord said it's not good to be commanded in all things. Sometimes we have to do things out of our own free will and choice, so I'm doing things on my own free will and choice."

"Floyd," she said, "you don't have to worry about that. It's none of your business. I'm keeping Rhondo in the mission field."

"I'm sorry," I said. "I didn't know that. But I've got this . . ."

"We don't want it," she said. "I'll keep him in the mission field."

And she did.

I didn't send him one penny.

He came home, and they got married. He went to law school and my last post card from them was from England. He recently was inducted into the BYU Athletic Hall of Fame. Rhondo stirred up the gift of God within himself and became an All-American wrestler and an All-Church missionary.

* * *

A few years ago we had an athlete here named Kevin Doman. He and Steve Lindsley, a quarterback here, played football together at Skyline High School in Salt Lake City and won the state championship. Both went to junior college and both went on missions. When Kevin returned, he decided to walk on to the team at BYU. He wasn't really given much hope of ever achieving or amounting to anything as an athlete. But he told me of a story he had once heard and kept in his thoughts at all times.

> A farmer had a pen of chickens. And in that pen of chickens was an eagle. But that eagle acted just like the chickens. It even began to make noises like the chickens. It went around scratching the ground, scouring for things to eat. It didn't realize it was a majestic eagle.
>
> One day a naturalist came along and spotted the eagle in the pen with the chickens. Surprised, he said to the farmer, "You have an eagle in that pen!"
>
> "No," the farmer said, "that's a chicken."
>
> "It's an eagle," the naturalist demanded.

The farmer told him that the bird had been in the pen for a long time. "It's nothing more than a chicken—just a chicken," he said.

The naturalist asked if he could take the eagle, and the farmer consented. The naturalist then took the eagle to the edge of a high cliff and said to the eagle, "Oh, eagle, thou art a great bird. Fly high! Freedom is yours! Sail the skies!"

The eagle just sat on his hand. It was a chicken.

He took the eagle back to the pen but returned the next day and once more took it to the cliff. He held the eagle on his arm and said, "Oh, eagle, destiny has meant for you to be king of all birds. Fly through the heavens! See the wonders of natures, for you are a king! Listen, oh eagle!"

The eagle fluttered its wings just a little, and then dropped its head. It didn't understand, for it was just a chicken.

The naturalist took the eagle back to the pen again, but returned the next day to take the eagle to the cliff. He repeated the procedure over and over. And each day he could see that there was a little more stirring within the eagle. So he held the eagle out and said, "Oh, eagle, look toward the heavens! There is the maker of all. You are not a chicken! You are not a chicken! You are an eagle! Your destiny is to be a king! To fly high! To sail through the boundaries of space! Happiness is your lot! Oh, eagle, eagle fly!"

And then the eagle began to flap his wings and slowly lifted into the heavens.

"I heard that story and realized that all my life I had been running around with kids who had no vision," Kevin told me. "They were nothing more than chickens scratching around on the ground for anything they could find. But I felt I had a mission to perform—just like that eagle. I was not a chicken. I was not an average bird. I wasn't going to lay any eggs. I was going to get up and fly like eagles and be what God wanted me to be."

Kevin didn't earn a football scholarship here until his senior year. He redshirted a year and played a year, and went on scholarship his senior year. When Coach Edwards put him on scholarship, he brought his wife back to see me and said, "I'm an eagle! I have reached what I wanted to reach."

Whenever we went on speaking engagements, Michelle would always tell the eagle story because Kevin's life was an example of what could be done by setting goals and working hard.

Kevin and Michelle moved into Wymount Terrace, the BYU student housing. But Kevin didn't want to hold down a job like other students, so he would buy a bunch of things like fire extinguishers, knives, etc., and hire his friends to go out and sell them. He would make a commission on everything they sold. He got his scholarship for his last year, but he made enough money in the summertime that he didn't really have to worry about money. He was an eagle. He was a guy who ruled the skies.

During June, Kevin went with me to speak at a big fireside in Reno, Nevada. A neurologist had invited us to speak, and Kevin sat by him at the dinner table. They began talking about Kevin's future. He was going to graduate in August of that year. Kevin told the doctor that his desire was to go to New York City to work on Wall Street.

A short while later, Kevin and Michelle made a trip to New York, and Kevin was offered a job on Wall Street. Two months after he got his job, however, the stock market crashed. Thousands of people lost their jobs, but not Kevin Doman. He was an eagle, and he had learned to fly. He's still working there. In addition, he's working on his Masters of Business Administration degree at New York University.

Kevin Doman knew how to stir up the gift of God within himself. He knew how to set goals and soar with the eagles. He is more proof that, once you realize you are a son or daughter of God, nothing is impossible—no dream is too grand.

* * *

Those who followed BYU's national championship team of 1984 will remember the name of Kelly Smith. He came out of Beaver, Utah. He walked on as a freshman and weighed a paltry 165 pounds.

Coaches around here are very kind. They'll almost let anybody try out for football who knows how many yards there are in a 100-yard dash. That's why they let Kelly try out.

You need to understand that if we have 50 walk-ons try out for the football team, five never dress out the first day. They get their locker and equipment but never show up for practice. And the first day after practice, five more will drop out. Because of injury or discouragement, about 10 more will drop out within the week. They get knocked around pretty good out there because they have to practice against the first-team players. We call them the Hamburger Squad. When you're on that squad, no one appreciates you very much. They think you look better lying on the ground than standing up.

And that's exactly how Kelly Smith was treated. But Kelly had something the other guys didn't have. He had a belief in himself. No one knew Kelly like Kelly knew Kelly. He believed there were some things he could do and some things the Lord would expect him to do. He wasn't going to disappoint himself or the Lord. He would give everything he could until he had proven he didn't have anything more to give.

Kelly Smith probably was one of the most inspirational players ever at BYU. He never did tip the scales at more than 180 pounds, and yet when we won the national championship in 1984, he was one of the leaders who inspired the rest of the team to live up to their potential. He came back from an injury and caught the winning touchdown pass in the Holiday Bowl that secured the national championship. He proved that a small kid from a small town could succeed just as well as the city kids.

All of these athletes I have mentioned in the chapter had two things in common: First, they believed in themselves. They believed they had ability. They believed they had talent. And they believed God expected them to perform to their very best because Christ was their strength. Second, they believed they had a mission, and with God's help, they would be able to perform that mission.

The Lord wants us to succeed. Satan—the opponent— sometimes seems to have the game won. But the odds are never too great to come back. We know God's team will be victorious when the final gun sounds. We just have to make sure we are on His team when the game ends.

5

Fumbled Opportunities

The preceding chapter was a testimonial to what can be accomplished if a person follows a dream and trusts in the Lord to help him accomplish that goal. We all love to hear about the athlete who, perhaps lacking the physical ability of the superstars, pushes on to success despite the odds. But for every one of those stories, there are a hundred stories of the athlete with seemingly limitless potential who, for whatever reason, fails to reach it. We don't usually hear much about those people because they have failed to magnify their talents, to develop their abilities. They have been handed the ball but have fumbled their opportunity.

I have discovered from my years of associating with athletes that there is a fine line between success and failure. Three ingredients seem to make a great athlete: 1) self discipline, 2) humility, and 3) a desire to succeed. When someone with a lot of potential fails to live up to expectations, you can usually trace their failure to a lack of one of those ingredients.

Consequently, recruiting athletes is a risky business. When a coach signs an athlete, he never knows what the end result is going to be. Too often, athletes with the greatest potential and the ones who received the greatest notoriety in high school do not prove to be great in college. Sometimes their talent is superior to any other athlete on the team, but the simple fact is that they don't have one or all of the ingredients necessary to become great. LaVell Edwards often has stated that "success does not always come to the most endowed." He admits that the best athletes often are the ones watching from the sidelines during the games. Someone once said that a great athlete is made of 80 percent desire, 15 percent talent, and five percent opportunity.

The first "principle of greatness" that athletes must possess is *self-discipline*. Another word for that is commitment. Life is not always easy for athletes who come to BYU. It is not your average university. Rules have been established to keep them from doing certain things. Sometimes there are rules upon rules designed to keep them in line. Athletes must be self-disciplined enough to be able to live with and accept those rules and not have the feeling of being restricted.

I've mentioned some BYU athletes who sneaked out on road trips and chased around town after the coach had gone to bed. They didn't have the self-discipline that it took for them to become great. And our football program showed it back then. We lost many more games than we won.

The same principle applies to the classroom and cheating. If a student studying medicine decides to cheat in college, that person will never become a great doctor. Likewise, if an athlete is lazy and expects things to be handed to him and thinks he does not need to work on the practice field, he will rarely attain greatness.

When people flounder because of a lack of self discipline, selfishness usually is at the root of their failure. Self-discipline is the most common problem in most of our failure—not only in athletics, but also in marriage, in business, and in our own families. Worst of all, lack of self-discipline creates a lack of self-respect. I've never seen a kid who has come here and failed who has had a high opinion of himself.

* * *

In the late '60s and early '70s we had a young man come to play basketball who was 7 feet tall and still growing. At that time, he was one of the real great prospects we had ever signed. You just didn't pick up a 7-footer every day back then. He became interested in the church after he got to BYU, and was baptized by the next spring. But his testimony was like the seed that falls on rocky soil and springs up quick and then dies when the sun beats down on it.

In the fall of his sophomore year, he came into the equipment room and said, "Security police sure are dumb around here."

"What?" I asked, surprised by his comment.

"I have over $250 in parking tickets, and they are trying to get my car so they can impound it until I pay," he said. "But I'm too smart for them."

"How do you get to school?" I asked. "Do you walk or drive your car?"

"I walk to school," he replied. "I'm not going to let them get my car."

"How far do you live from campus?" I asked.

"A couple of miles or so."

"And you walk to campus every morning?"

"Yes, I walk every morning."

"And after practice at night you walk home?" I asked.

"Sure, how else would I get there?" he smiled.

I shook my head and said, "Now you do all this walking— between four and five miles a day—because the University Police are dumb?"

He nodded. "I'm too smart for them."

That nonsense went on until about the middle of November. In that day and age, athletes had to have their professors sign an eligibility slip saying that academically the players were eligible to travel. Well, this athlete thought that process would be a waste of time, so he sat in his room and forged his professors' signatures on the slip.

It didn't take the coach long to realize that the signatures weren't those of the professors, so he called the player in to his office. The athlete laughed about it and readily confessed that he had forged the signatures. He said he did it to save the professors trouble.

The coach put him on probation and suspended him from practice for a couple of weeks. He came back to practice on a Wednesday sometime in December. The following Sunday, we got a call from his mother saying they had found her son's car in Battle Mountain, Nevada, but could find no sign of him. She was wondering if he was on campus. We checked his dormitory, but the bed had not been slept in. He couldn't be found anyplace.

To this day, we don't know what happened to that athlete. He was blessed with that ingredient you can't coach—height but he lacked the self-discipline to accept and live within the rules and the laws necessary for success.

Anyone who is going to be successful in athletics must first learn to discipline himself, then the rules and laws he is living under won't bother him because he is not rubbing against them. The same applies to the commandments in the Church. If we live the commandments, we have perfect free agency to achieve and to grow and to do the things we ought to be doing.

We have had several athletes over the years with All-America potential who, for various reasons, amounted to nothing. The greatest way I know for anyone to become a nothing is to live without self discipline. Those people just fade into the distance. Nobody wants anything to do with them. No success comes into their lives.

Way back when I first started here when we didn't win many games, I remember a couple of players standing on the sidelines during a game. They were trying to figure out how to get the quarterback and, if possible, injure him. They hatched a plan and decided they were going to put the quarterback out of the game because he was the key player for the other team. Rather than improve their own play, they were trying to eliminate the guy who was giving them the most trouble. That's a lack of self-discipline.

They failed in their mission. In fact, they ended up hurting themselves. You see too much fighting, too much trying to hurt the opponent, even in pro ball. These mammoth athletes are taking swings at each other during the games. Tell me, how are you going to hurt someone who is wearing shoulder pads, a helmet, a facemask, and hip pads? I don't care how hard you fight. Anyone who fights another football player is only going to hurt himself.

* * *

In 1941, I finished attending classes at BYU in June. I had not served a mission, although that was one of my life's dreams. I was getting to be an old man of 23 years. An older brother of mine had served a mission, and I knew that I had to go then if I was going to serve. War was threatening. Canada and England already were at war with Germany.

At that time, a new Utah State Prison was being built at the Point of the Mountain. My older brother was working there, and he encouraged me to go with him to see if I could find work. I agreed, and the next morning hitch-hiked to Pleasant Grove, where I caught a ride with him to the state prison. I didn't take a lunch or anything. I didn't have much optimism.

When we arrived, I was standing around the construction site watching the laborers work on the buildings. The foreman came over. He was busy, and didn't have time to talk to me. He went over to a big guy named Hans and said, "Send us up some cement."

"We haven't got anybody in the sand and gravel," Hans shouted back.

I was standing there doing nothing and decided I might as well help them out. I walked over to the big guy and asked how many wheelbarrows of sand and how many of gravel he needed. He informed me that he needed three loads of sand and two of gravel. I grabbed a shovel and went to work.

Before I had finished the first wheelbarrow, he turned to me and said, "Are you a member of the union?"

"No," I replied, "just a member of the Deseret Sunday School Union."

Of course, he didn't understand what that meant, and he said, "Well, then, you can't work here if you're not a union member."

"I haven't even been hired," I said. "They asked for cement, and you can't make it without sand and gravel. I'll just supply you with sand and gravel so you can do your part."

I didn't pay any attention to him and just kept working. After about 45 minutes, the foreman came back. He said, "Has anyone hired you?"

"No sir," I said, "but I heard you ask that fellow over there for cement and he has to have sand and gravel before he can get cement."

"You're hired," he said.

By that time, my hands were raw. I had no gloves on. Pretty soon, a young man I had known at BYU came down to help me. I asked him whether he would rather shovel sand or gravel. He chose the sand because it was easier.

All that day we made and poured cement. By the end of the day, my hands were nothing but red meat. I went up to the boss and said, "This guy at the cement mixer keeps telling me I've got to be with the union."

"Don't pay any attention to him," the boss admonished. "Utah is a right-to-work state, so you don't have to belong to the union."

The next day I returned to work (with gloves) but they took me off the cement mixer and put me up on the vibrator. The vibrator was a machine designed to make sure no air pockets were inside the walls.

Prisoners were not allowed to come inside the construction zone, but they were out in the compound. There was no shade where we were working, and it was extremely hot, so my friend and I went over onto the compound to find some shade during lunch.

We were sitting there eating when an old man dressed in striped overalls and sporting a crew-cut came over and asked if he could talk to us. His face had been weather-beaten by the sun and wind and rain. We could see he was herding cows.

I was apprehensive about the prisoners because I had never been around any before. He looked at us and then asked, "What do you plan on doing with your lives?"

"We are going on missions for the LDS Church this fall," we answered.

"Can I give you a bit of advice?" he asked.

How many times in your life do you get advice from a prisoner? So we said, "Sure!"

"They call me Doc," he began. "I am a doctor of medicine. Here, I'm a cow herder. I drive cows. See these hands? They were hands prepared to perform delicate operations. Now they hold sticks that I drive cows with. That's because when I was a little older than you, I did not learn one important thing: that laws were set up to preserve liberty. I wanted to be a law unto myself. I could not discipline myself.

"I performed operations that were illegal, and I had a patient die. Now I am here for life. And out of that life sentence, I already have served 30 years. Look at my hands!"

They were wrinkled and cracked and weather-beaten.

"These were prepared for delicate operations, and because I lacked the ability to discipline myself, I've never been able to be of service to mankind.

"There are two other things I want to tell you fellahs. One is that you can do anything that you want to do if you really want to do it. You just have to believe in yourself. The other thing is that you may think that you know everything, but you don't. And when you get the way I was, you think you have all the knowledge there is to get. Just don't believe you know everything because you don't know anything yet."

That fall we went into the mission field. And two years later, when I returned, I went with my brother to the prison dairy shortly after I got back. I was anxious to see how the construction had progressed.

The first person I saw when I got there was Doc. His face was a little more wrinkled. His hair was a little whiter. And as I stepped out of the truck, he saw me and remembered me. He came limping up to me, grabbed my hand and said, "You're been, and you're back."

"Yes," I said, "I've been, and I'm back."

He said, "Did you remember what I told you?"

I was happy to say that I had, indeed, remembered his counsel. And I told him that it had been one of the sources of inspiration for my mission.

"Remember that all your life," he said. "Learn the difference between right and wrong and gather the strength to do the right. Never think that you ever have learned everything, because someone is going to trip you up. Always remember that you can be anything you want to be if you want to be it bad enough."

Old Doc's advice has remained a part of me throughout my life. I'll never forget looking at those wrinkled hands and the invaluable lesson they taught.

* * *

Another key ingredient athletes must have to be successful is *humility*. Since life is a school where we are to learn to be better men and women, it's amazing how hard it is for some people to learn the ability to succeed, and yet how easy it is for others to learn the same principle. Some people are completely unteachable. Not because they are stupid but because they have no humility. Humility is teachability.

Any athlete who goes to the coach and says, "Here I am. I want to learn," can be taught. But too often athletes have the feeling—particularly if they were highly recruited high school athletes—that they know everything.

I once taught a Sunday School class of 15-year-olds. When the bishop called me to the position, he took me into his office and told me they were good kids and that they were the children of very successful men—professors, businessmen, and the like.

"This is June, and you're going to be the seventh teacher they've had since January," he said, hoping I wouldn't turn around and walk out (or pass out).

I knew some of the kids in the class, and I agreed to do it.

I went into my new class the next Sunday and met eleven 15-to-16-year-old kids. There were five boys and six girls. One boy was standing at the blackboard and had drawn seven stick figures. He had drawn crosses through six of the figures and had half an X drawn through the seventh when I walked in. I stood there in the doorway, but no one paid attention to me. There was a little table by the door, so I decided to make a dramatic entry. I took the flat of my hand and slapped it down on the table so that the resulting noise sounded like a gun going off. Everybody turned around and looked at me.

"Hi, I'm your teacher," I announced with a smile.

I then turned to the young man at the blackboard and said, "Jay, I didn't know you're an artist." (Really, those were the most pathetic stick men I had ever seen.)

"Well," he said, obviously proud of his work, "I've just been keeping score of how many teachers we've had."

"You mean I'm that guy over there with half a cross through him?"

He nodded and said, "Yep. You won't want to stay in here with us."

"You wanna bet?" I said. "Hey, I'm here to stay. You're hereby retired as score keeper. We don't need any score keepers in this class."

Then I asked them to tell me why they came to Sunday School. They weren't bashful about naming four reasons: 1) their parents made them; 2) there was no other place to go; 3) they had a chance to visit with their friends; and 4) once in a while they learned something.

"Only once in a while you learn something?" I asked.

"We know it already," they declared. "We get the stuff in seminary, then we come here and get it all over again. It's boring. We know it all!"

It wasn't hard to see they lacked humility.

"Well," I proclaimed, "I just had a vision. You are the first bunch that I've ever met that knows it all. So if you really know everything, I'm not going to be your teacher, I'm going to be your motivator, and you're going to do just exactly what I ask you to do."

To tell the truth, I didn't really know what I was going to do. But I had other visions during the week. I called every rest home in Utah Valley, including the State Training School and the State Mental Hospital, to find out who conducted their meetings and who I should call to arrange for that class to bless and pass the sacrament for the patients and to do the praying and lead the singing. I decided to take those kids every Sunday afternoon to visit rest homes.

The first Sunday we went to a rest home in Orem, and I told the kids that these were very lonely people. I mentioned that on Sunday the women had hairdressers come in to help them get all fixed up for their Sunday meetings. I asked the class members to be friendly because sometimes those people are completely forgotten.

"Tell them how nice they look. It might be hard to tell them you love them, but at least give some encouraging word. Shake their hands afterward," I encouraged.

We organized who was going to do the talking, the praying, the singing, and the sacrament, and then went to the rest home.

We had a great service. The patients loved it. Afterwards, I went around shaking the hands of all the patients and talking to them, but when I turned around, my Sunday School class had disappeared. I went out to the cars and found them waiting for me.

"What are you doing?" I asked.

"We are waiting for you," they explained.

"But I told you to go around and shake the peoples' hands and talk to them and tell them how nice they look."

"We didn't want to do that," they said.

Still no sign of humility.

Two weeks later, we went to a rest home in Provo. I told the kids that they were going to have one of the greatest honors they could ever imagine. Our accompanist would be one of Utah's greatest musicians ever, Florence Jefferson Madsen. She was a patient there, and she had agreed to accompany us. But the kids weren't impressed. They didn't know who she was and didn't really care.

We made our plans and went to the rest home. There were about 30 women, all dressed up and pretty. After the meeting, I went around shaking their hands, telling them how happy we were to be there and how nice they all looked. Someone nudged me, and I turned around and saw all my kids lined up behind me. They were shaking hands and talking to the patients. Finally, they had caught the spirit of humility.

A couple of weeks later, we went to the State Training School in American Fork. About 350 patients were in that congregation, all with handicaps. Some of them were 30 or 40 years of age. As we got out of the cars, one of the patients standing nearby asked, "These all your kids, Mister?"

"Yes," I smiled, "these are all my kids."

"Boy, you sure got a lot of kids," he said.

We made our way into the Sacrament Meeting. They had a choir that was made up of about 40 patients. Some of them were in their 40s or 50s. Three of the kids were going to do the speaking. The choir started the meeting off by singing "Jesus Wants Me For A Sunbeam." My kids looked at those patients in that choir and noticed that they were putting everything they had into that song.

There was hardly a dry eye among my kids as we left that meeting, and I began to notice a change that was coming into their lives. They had discovered that they really didn't know everything. They had experienced humility.

That was several years ago. We ended up with 18 kids in that class. Every boy and every girl attended regularly, plus we picked up a couple who weren't supposed to be there, and a couple from another ward. Every boy from that group went on a mission and married in the temple. Every girl married in the temple except one, and that one gal still hasn't married.

Those kids, who had been so caught up in themselves, learned to share of themselves, to believe in themselves, and to be humble. The result was an outstanding group of young people devoted to our Heavenly Father.

* * *

I had a bishop once who, in a talk, told about the buffalo that roamed the plains. The buffalo usually wandered in herds. Sometimes the herds were rather small. If one of the small herds was confronted by danger, the buffalo would form a circle by putting their tails together and pointing their heads outward. Coyotes, wolves, and other predators couldn't get them because the only way to disable them was to get hold of the hamstring or the juggler vein. The buffalo were protected by the circle of massive heads ready to fend off their enemies.

Every once in a while, however, a young yearling probably thought to himself, "Isn't that a stupid thing to see those big animals standing in a circle with their hind ends touching? I don't need that kind of protection. I'm going to do it on my own."

When that yearling got surrounded by a pack of wolves, he soon discovered he couldn't protect himself at all. While one predator was after his juggler vein, another was back snapping at his hamstring. Eventually, the yearling went down to become a meal for the hungry wolves.

Teamwork was necessary for the buffalo, and it is essential for a successful football team. It's also a necessity for families, who must learn to protect and to love and to live for each other. Athletics, families, business—it all works with the same principle. You must have humility or you're not going to succeed.

* * *

The last principle necessary for success is the *desire to succeed*. Sometimes that desire is one of the hardest things to keep and maintain. Occasionally, people have a problem with their self-image. When that happens, desire for success diminishes. And sometimes they have a problem with humility, which results in a drop in their desire to succeed. We must continually keep the desire for success kindled.

As I mentioned earlier, success is made of 80 percent desire, 15 percent talent, and 5 percent opportunity. Whether that is totally accurate could be debated. We do know, however, that behind every successful athlete, or behind any successful endeavor, is a tremendous desire to achieve.

The Lord said that if you have desires to serve Him, you are called to His service (D&C 4:3). In the Fourth Section of the Doctrine and Covenants, He gave Joseph Smith one of the first principles to help him be successful as a prophet and get the kingdom growing. That principle was to have a *desire*.

If you have desires to serve Him, then you are called to His service.

Notice how there is nothing said about talent, time, looks, or feelings as prerequisites to serve the Lord. The Lord wants people with DESIRE. There are at least two or three references in the Doctrine and Covenants wherein the Lord says, "If you have a desire to serve, thrust in your sickle and reap." To see your desires come to fruition, you must be willing to work hard—to thrust in your sickle, if you will.

I related the story of Chuck Cutler in a previous chapter. Chuck had the desire, but he didn't have all the talent. He had self-discipline and was very teachable. But he also had the desire to be successful and to go out and speak to the youth. He knew that he would be more persuasive if he had a recognizable name and impressive accomplishments to back up his words. He knew it would mean more if he had been successful. He worked his heart out to achieve that success.

And consider Mike Smith or Andy Toolson or Marty Haws. Most of the fans don't know what happens to those players from one ballgame to the next. They don't know that when Andy Toolson misses a 3-point shot, he carries that disappointment with him throughout the week. The desire to succeed creates within him a desire to practice. I've seen him out there for hours at a time standing around the three-point circle pumping shot after shot. His desire to be successful has stimulated a determination to work hard.

Mike Smith finished his career as the best free throw shooter in the history of NCAA Division I basketball. He did it by working hour after hour shooting free throw after free throw. Mike Smith has the desire to achieve.

I have a list of every football player who has played at BYU for the last 25 years. I can show you the ones who failed and the ones who succeeded. Pretty much every one of the failures lacked one of the ingredients. They were not self-disciplined, they were not teachable, or they didn't have the desire to achieve. You cannot have success without all three ingredients.

Elder Paul H. Dunn has said, "When you see a man standing on a mountain, you know he didn't just drop there." He had to get up there somehow. And when you see an All-American, you know someone didn't just hand him a certificate with his name inscribed on it. He's got to work hard to become an All-American. If he has the self-discipline, the humility, and the desire to succeed, his ability to conquer things in this world will be almost beyond his own imagination.

It's a great thing to be an All-American. But it's an even greater thing to be an All-Mormon whose desire is to serve and touch the lives of other people. The Lord expects us to utilize the talents we have. He has handed us the ball. Now it's our job not to fumble it.

6

Down and Out

S ome of the most discouraged people I have ever seen in
my life have been kids being carried off the football field
with career-ending injuries. They felt like everyone had aban-
doned them, including the Lord. All their dreams had gone
out the window. But in the end, everyone of them, almost
without exception, found a dream they had never imagined.

* * *

I don't want to use a name on this story because it's one
that has deeply affected me as I've seen the change that
has come into this young man's life. He came here as a junior
college transfer. He was an arrogant kid; not LDS. In fact,
he was not very religious at all. The players didn't accept him
very well. I spent time talking with him because he needed
someone to speak to.

During his first year at BYU, he suffered a knee injury that put him out for the season. Then the next spring he suffered a shoulder injury that kept him out of spring practice. He spent the entire summer rehabilitating and getting ready to play football. But the bad luck continued, and he injured his other knee in the fall.

"Why do I have all the bad luck?" this young man asked me a dozen times.

"I really don't know," was my answer. "Maybe the Lord is trying to tell you something, but you're not listening."

"Why doesn't he just come out and say it in plain words," he wondered out loud.

"Because sometimes we won't listen and won't hear. Sometimes we have to suffer adversities."

"Do you remember learning about Joseph Smith?" I asked.

"Oh, a little bit," he said.

"There was a time in his life when he thought the whole world was against him. He and a couple of leaders of the Church were in a prison called Liberty. He was deprived of his family, and fed meat that wasn't fit for dogs to eat. He got to a low point in his life and, for the first time that I know about, he complained to the Lord and said, 'Where art thou? Where art thou?' He was feeling a lot like you are right now. And do you know what the answer was to him?"

"The Lord said to him, 'My son, peace be unto thy soul.' (D&C 121:7-8).

"You're not getting that message because you don't know Him very well. Joseph Smith heard the Lord because he knew Him. And then the Lord said, 'Thine adversity and thine afflictions shall be but a small moment; and then if thou endure it well, God shall exalt thee on high; thou shalt triumph over all thy foes.' (D&C 121)"

"God is saying that same thing to you, only you don't know him well enough to be able to receive that and to understand it."

"How do I get that way?" he asked.

"By prayer. And by preparation and study so you can get to know Him and His ways. Find out what He wants you to do. You have no concept about why you are here on Earth and here at BYU. You think you're here to be a football hero. And yet you are not going to become that. Already the Lord has rebuffed you three times. So you better find out what he wants you to do."

"How do I do that?" he asked again.

"You pray, and you study. The first thing you've got to do is get to know your Heavenly Father."

I don't know how many times he came into my office after that so we could talk and pray about these things. Soon Christmas was approaching. I knew little about his family situation back in the East. His mother was divorced. He had a sister, to whom he had given a black eye the last time they had been together. He and his mother hadn't had a good relationship. But there had been so much growth in him that fall that he had decided to go home. Joseph Smith now was a prophet to him. God was real. Jesus was an older brother, the Son of God, the Redeemer. He understood those things but not totally and completely. Still, they were becoming part of his life, and when I talked to him about them, it wasn't like I was speaking in a foreign tongue.

He came to see me a few days before Christmas and said, "I'm going home for Christmas. I don't know what my mother will do, but I'm going home. I want to see my mom and sister. My sister's married."

It was only a few days after Christmas when he came back again.

"What are you doing here?" I asked. "I thought you were going home for Christmas."

"I did. But I've got to get those missionaries. I've got to hear those lessons."

I asked what had happened at home to bring about this desire.

He said, "I got home at dusk and took a taxi to where my mom lives. I rang the doorbell, not knowing how she was going to receive me because our communication hasn't been very good over the years. She opened the door, and just stood there. I opened my arms and said, 'Mom, I love you so darn much!'"

"She started crying and rushed into my arms, and we embraced right there in the doorway. She wanted to know what had happened—why I had changed so drastically. I explained to her the things that I had been going through.

"Then I went over to see my sister. I didn't know what kind of reception I would receive. I had left her with a black eye the last time we were together. I wondered whether she was going to give me one the moment she saw me.

"I rang the doorbell. She opened the door, looked at me, and took a step back. I said, 'It's me, your brother. I'm here to tell you how much I love you.' She hesitated a minute, then came rushing into my arms. We began talking, and the more I talked to her about the changes that had come into my life, the more the desire was built up that I had to get back to Utah and get the missionaries because I didn't have time to wait another minute! Can I see the missionaries tonight?" he asked.

I told him I wasn't sure if I could track them down. But I finally reached them and asked if they would get in touch with this young man as soon as possible. He called me at 10 o'clock that night and said they still hadn't called him. I told him to go to sleep, and I would get hold of them in the morning.

"Can't you call them tonight?" he begged.

It took us two days to finally hook up with the missionaries. And then he was baptized into the Church.

This young man, who was hoping to be an all-star football player, found another mission here at BYU. And nearly every story about young men whose careers are cut short by injury or illness ends the same way: God becomes the central figure in their life, Jesus becomes the main character, whose influence is felt the greatest in their lives; the Church becomes the teaching tool that brings them close to Heavenly Father and Jesus.

The young man of the story is completely content. He's a member of the Church, and the last I heard, serving in a bishopric. He thought he had lost his life when he was injured; yet in reality he found life because he was willing to reach out and grab the gospel as support.

* * *

At the conclusion of the 1977 season, the football team was on its way to Japan and stopped in Hawaii to play a football game. While we were there, Coach Edwards pulled all the guys together for a team meeting. No one had any idea what it was about. Brian Hansen, a linebacker from American Fork, Utah, had gone with us on the trip but wasn't at the meeting.

Coach Edwards told us that Brian had just found out he had multiple sclerosis, a very serious illness that often results in partial or complete paralysis. Every football player on that team felt humbled and concerned. Coach Edwards then asked the entire team to get on their knees and pray for Brian. There was no hesitation by anyone—even the non-members on the team dropped to their knees and called upon God to intervene for Brian.

We tried not to treat Brian differently than we previously had, but we all felt in our hearts a sympathy and love going out to him. We loved the big guy, and we had been asked to help heal him.

The team flew on to Japan. Brian went along but did not dress with the team or play in any of the games. A short while after we returned, I learned that Brian had accepted a mission call and was in the mission field. As best I remember, he had one flareup with the disease in the mission field but was healthy from then on.

Brian's difficulty brought him closer to our Heavenly Father and certainly brought the members of our football team closer together because of their love for Brian and because they had joined their faith in Brian's behalf.

Brian later became a starting linebacker and a three-year letterman. His big, powerful muscles, once threatened by a dangerous disease, brought down many a running back. Brian was lucky. He got a second chance at football. As he faced his crisis with courage and faith, the entire team benefited from the experience.

* * *

Kirk Davis is another young man whose courage and determination inspired the team and the thousands of fans who followed his story. Kirk transferred to BYU from Ricks College, where he was a second-team All-American in football.

He earned a spot as a backup defensive back his first year at BYU. Rodney Rice, the starter ahead of Kirk, injured an elbow in the Texas game, opening the door for Kirk to get some real playing time. In fact, he got to start the following week against TCU.

BYU got beat up pretty good by Texas Christian that week, and the defensive backfield was no exception. The next day, Kirk noticed a lump on his neck and showed it to the trainers. They were concerned and asked that he see the team doctor.

The next day   only two days after getting his first starting assignment in major college football—the doctors told Kirk he had Hodgkins Disease, a form of cancer. The good news, if you could call it that, was that the cancer was still in stage one and probably could be treated.

Imagine the agony Kirk endured as he shared the information with his wife, who was expecting their first child. Football seemed trivial now that his life was at risk. Nevertheless, Kirk went to Coach Edwards and told him the doctors had

given him permission to continue playing football if he
wanted to.

"The team needs me, and I will continue to play," he said.

He started the next week against New Mexico and returned
an intercepted pass for a touchdown. Then doctors performed
more tests and determined they had to remove Kirk's spleen.

The defensive backfield was still riddled with injury, so
Kirk begged the doctors to let him wait until after the Home-
coming game two weeks later to undergo surgery. They
consented.

Kirk had his spleen removed and had radiation to stop the
cancer. He lost 20 pounds and felt like he had a constant case
of the flu for several months.

During that time, he would come into the office and say,
"Do you have any speaking assignments? Is there anything
I can do? I need to be busy."

He went out many times and shared his testimony with
young people. "I give lots of talks," he once told a reporter.
"I don't want kids to take life for granted. One unexpected
thing like this can really change your life. We all need to take
time to smell the roses."

Kirk's battle with cancer seems to be over. He was the
victor. Like Brian Hansen, Kirk got to finish his last year of
football. But his decision to stay with the team and contribute
what he could, even though a major crisis had occurred in his
life, was a true inspiration to all of us who knew him and the
struggles he was going through.

* * *

Gifford Nielsen was the leading candidate for the Heisman Trophy four games into the 1977 season. He
hadn't thrown an interception in the first three games, and all
the networks were drooling over his every pass. BYU was
undefeated and ranked higher than they ever had been before.
Reporters from the East were hailing him as the Heisman

frontrunner, and some had practically handed the trophy to him, even though there were still seven games to play.

The fourth game was at Oregon State. It was a tight game, and Gifford suffered a knee injury in the second half. Gifford was carried to the sidelines and placed on the bench, where he put his face in a towel to hide the pain and the disappointment. Gifford's dream of a Heisman Trophy had just been dashed, along with the hopes of what looked to be a promising professional career.

When we got back to Provo, Giff's knee was operated on and he was told he would be out for the season. He had every reason in the world to be bitter, but there was no bitterness in Gifford Nielsen. Marc Wilson, his backup, stepped in the following week and broke an NCAA record for the most touchdown passes.

The eastern media soon forgot Gifford, and the Heisman Trophy went to a running back named Earl Campbell. Many wondered whether Gifford would ever play pro ball since the pros are always cautious when it comes to drafting injured players.

Yet the Houston Oilers gambled and selected Gifford in the third round of the NFL draft. He became a popular player with his teammates and the Houston fans. Perhaps the highlight of his professional career came when he stepped in for the starting quarterback, who was injured, and led the Oilers to a playoff victory. A few years later, he retired to become a sportscaster in Houston. He is still a celebrity in Houston and is an excellent ambassador for the Church. What better way to spread the gospel than by television?

Gifford could have cursed God for preventing him from receiving the fame and glory that were certainly going to be heaped upon him at the end of his college career. He could have given up and decided the injury was a sign for him to do something else. But Gifford never murmured against his Heavenly Father. He never gave up.

Today, he is a member of the BYU Athletic Hall of Fame and, if there were such a thing, he would be a charter member of the Courage Hall of Fame.

* * *

I call Danny Frazier my son. I'll never forget him. He came here in 1977. He was black and a member of the Church. He was originally from Arizona, where he had been baptized. The family later moved to Tooele, Utah. From there he came to BYU.

Danny was good friends with a young man named Scott Rebber, who hailed from St. George. Scott was a free-spirited kid. Danny was a good kid, but he hadn't yet learned to fulfill responsibility, as is the case with most freshmen.

After they had been at BYU for six weeks, I asked them to speak at a seminary morningside in American Fork. Scott and I weren't exactly friends because he had a tumbleweed haircut when he showed up for workouts, and I wouldn't give him a helmet until he cut it. He played three days without a helmet before his head got a little sore, and he decided to get a hair cut.

Our appointment to speak was at 6:30 on a Wednesday morning. Danny and Scott were supposed to meet me at my office, but they didn't show up, so I had to face that group of seminary students by myself.

When I got back to my office, I called a couple of the cheerleaders I knew and asked them if they would like to speak at a seminary in Payson the following week. They said they would love to.

"Here's what I would like you to do," I told them. "There are a couple of football players I would like you to pick up on the way to the high school. They should have gone with me this morning, but they didn't. They still owe me a speaking engagement, and I'm going to hold them to it."

I gave them the address of the players and told them the time to pick them up the following Wednesday.

Later that same morning, Danny Frazier came waltzing into the locker room and went straight to his locker. He wisely avoided the equipment room because he knew what was in store if he showed his face to me. But I happened to see him and waited for a few minutes before confronting him.

"Hi, Dan," I said when I finally decided to call him to repentance.

"Oh, hi," he said, looking everywhere but into my eyes.

"Missed you this morning."

"Oh, yeah, my alarm clock didn't go off."

"You promised me you would go. Remember?"

"Sure, I'd have gone if my alarm clock had gone off," he argued.

"I've got it fixed up, Dan," I said. "Next week you're going to Payson."

"Payson?" he said.

"We're going to spend all day over there, and you are responsible for the class period between nine and ten o'clock. And so that you have a way to get over there, I have arranged for a cheerleader to pick you up. She'll take you in her car. You won't have to worry about your alarm clock."

"A cheerleader is taking me?" he asked.

"Yes, a cheerleader," I replied. "You're in good company. You definitely won't be ashamed of her."

About 1:30 that same day, Scott Rebber snuck into the locker room. He dressed further away from my office than Danny, but I saw him and walked over to him.

"Scott," I said, "I missed you this morning."

Of course, they had collaborated on their stories.

"Yeah, my alarm clock didn't go off."

"I thought it was Danny's alarm clock that didn't go off," I said.

"Oh, yeah, it was Danny's alarm clock that didn't go off."

"Well," I said, "I still feel like you owe me a promise. So I arranged for you to speak in Payson next Wednesday at 10 o'clock. You don't have to worry about your alarm clock or anything because I've arranged for one of the cheerleaders to pick you up and take you over there.

"A cheerleader?"

"You know. The girls who lead the cheers at football games. The ones you ogle at while you are supposed to be watching the football game. She'll come to your apartment to pick you up."

That next Wednesday, a cheerleader picked Danny up and took him to Payson. Then the other cheerleader picked up Scott and took him.

Danny was the first one back. He walked into my office and said, "That's the greatest feeling I've ever had."

"Did you have a good companion to speak with?" I asked, knowing already what the answer would be.

"Oh, yes. She was really pretty," Danny smiled.

An hour later, Scott showed up and said exactly the same thing. "Every time you give of yourself to help another person, it always helps you," I told them.

I reminded them what Edward Martin said:

"There is a destiny that makes us brothers,

And none goes his way alone.

All we give into the lives of others,

Comes back into our own."

We had a good season in football that year. The following year, the coaches decided to redshirt Danny Frazier. It was in June of 1978 when I heard about the revelation that all worthy males could hold the priesthood. Nothing in my life has electrified me like that.

The very next day, Danny Frazier poked his head around the corner and said, "Floyd, do you think I ought to go on a mission?"

"Do you hold the priesthood yet?" I asked.

He said he didn't.

"Do you have a mission call?"

He said he didn't.

"Then I don't think you ought to go on a mission," I said. But I told him that I felt he definitely ought to go on a mission someday.

That year Danny and I often talked about missions. We became very close.

The following year, Danny came back ready to play. He was a big, beautiful black athlete with a body that would have made Atlas jealous. He stood about 6-foot-5 and weighed about 225 pounds. He played linebacker in football and also played on the varsity basketball team for a season or two. He was a sure bet for a professional contract. It was practically money in the bank.

The very first game of his sophomore season was against Texas A&M. The game was played at Rice Stadium because Texas A&M's stadium was being expanded and hadn't yet been finished. It was a big game for BYU.

During the game, Danny and another linebacker named Glen Redd closed in on a running back to make a tackle. Their heads collided, and Danny fell to the ground. He was helped up and made his way over to the sideline before the pain really hit. The doctors told him he had a couple of crushed vertebrae in his back.

They laid him on a stretcher and took him to the hospital for X-rays. Then they put him on an airplane and flew him back to Salt Lake City, where he was expected to undergo emergency surgery at St. Mark's Hospital.

His career was ruined.

As he lay in the hospital, I tried repeatedly to reach him on the phone. But it was useless. His number was finally taken off the listing so people wouldn't keep calling.

The doctors operated on his back to fuse four or five vertebrae.

In the meantime, his family had moved from Tooele to Provo. Danny came home from the hospital and called me after a couple of days. "Floyd, do you think I ought to go on a mission?" he asked.

"Dan, we've talked about this before," I reminded him. "We had it all set up, but you lost interest when school started. Now the Lord has allowed you to break your back in order to open your ears. If you don't listen to Him now, I don't know what's going to happen to you next time."

Two weeks later we were playing football against the University of Hawaii in Provo. I was standing on the sidelines and looked up in time to see Danny—that big, handsome man who was now wearing a neck brace—walking along the edge of the field. I went over and started talking to him.

"I'm going on a mission," he told me. "I have an interview with my bishop this afternoon. We're going to start filling out the papers."

Three weeks later, Danny dropped by my office to tell me he had been called to the California Oakland Mission. He was thrilled with the possibility of going there to preach the gospel.

I promised Danny I would send him some BYU T-shirts to give to every person he taught on his mission. That nearly resulted in my financial ruin. I sent 250 T-shirts that year. The kid just about broke me. But just when I was beginning to doubt that I was going to be able to keep my promise, Danny was called into the mission office. My bank account was saved!

In January of 1981, we were having a big reception to honor the team after the Miracle Bowl. That was where BYU beat Southern Methodist in the Holiday Bowl on a last-second pass. Elder Dunn was there, and he had recently been out to the Oakland Mission.

"Did you happen to see Elder Frazier there?" I asked.

"Did I see him?" he laughed. "I couldn't miss him! We had a meeting there with at least 5,000 people. The missionaries brought their investigators, and I called Elder Frazier out of the audience to share his testimony. He tried to hide behind a little elder in front of him, but that big body just couldn't be hidden.

"He slowly made his way to the front and stood behind that pulpit and had a look of consternation and deep thought on his face. Then from his lips came the most beautiful testimony you could ever imagine. He bore testimony of the Savior and of His mission. He spoke of the gospel of repentance that he was teaching. And he said there was no football thrill in all the world that could compare with the thrill of teaching the gospel to someone who had ears to hear and eyes to see."

Danny completed a wonderful mission. And when he came back he still had a tremendous desire to play football. But that was out of the question. One doctor had told me that out of every 100 accidents like Danny's, 80 would have ended up in paralysis for the victim. There was no chance he could play football, and there was no place on the BYU basketball team for him, either.

He eventually received an offer to play basketball at BYU-Hawaii. He finished up there and applied for admission into the J. Reuben Clark Law School at BYU. He wasn't a great student, but he was accepted. Later he married a beautiful girl from St. Johns, Newfoundland, and graduated from Law School in the spring of 1989.

Danny was a great athlete who was destined for a bright professional career before he was wiped out by one untimely tackle. Although he gave up a promising football career, he gained something even greater. He went on a mission. He married a beautiful girl, and they have four little boys and one girl. In fact, Danny would not trade anything he has now for a pro career. For some reason, he was not to be a pro athlete. The Lord had other things for him to do.

The lesson I have learned from Danny Frazier's experience is that when the Lord closes one door, He usually opens another that leads to even greater blessings. Had Danny not suffered that injury, he probably never would have gone on a mission and never married the beautiful gal he did.

* * *

Every one of these young men suffered a major setback in their lives. But they discovered that the Lord often uses such trials to bless them. They now understand what the Lord was talking about when he told the Prophet Joseph Smith: "Thine adversity and thine afflictions shall be but a small moment; and then if thou endure it well, God will exalt thee on high."